The Stations of the Eucharist From Melchizedek to the Book of Revelation

By Denise Mercado

The Stations of the Eucharist:
From Melchizedek to the Book of Revelation
by Denise Mercado

Copyright 2025 Denise Mercado

All rights reserved. No portion of this book may be reproduced in any form without permission from the publisher except as permitted by U.S. copyright law. For permissions, contact denise@denisemercado.com

Cover design by James Hrkach of Innate Productions/Full Quiver Publishing; image of *Abraham y Melquisedec, por Juan Antonio de Frías* from Wikimedia Commons, public domain; and image of Ghent Altarpiece from Wikiart, public domain

Editing and Interior Design by
Ellen Gable of Innate Productions/Full Quiver Publishing

ISBN: 9798307687482
Printed in the United States of America

First Edition

NIHIL OBSTAT 11/13/2024
Very Reverend Joseph L. Waters
Censor Librorum
Diocese of St. Petersburg

Scripture texts in this work are taken from the *New American Bible, revised edition* © 2010, 1991, 1986, 1970 Confraternity of Christian Doctrine, Washington, D.C., and are used by permission of the copyright owner. All Rights Reserved. No part of the New American Bible may be reproduced in any form without permission in writing from the copyright owner.

Dedicated to my children and grandchildren

"Denise Mercado's book is a timely and profound exploration that bridges the rich tapestry of Old Testament covenants with their ultimate fulfillment in the New Testament. This book provides a transformative guide that takes the reader from head knowledge to heart devotion. By examining key biblical moments that prefigure the Eucharist, Mercado draws out the richness of God's eternal covenant, helping readers encounter the mystery of the Eucharist in a deeply personal way. This book is an invitation to not just learn about the Eucharist but to experience it as the spiritual nourishment God has provided throughout salvation history. A truly inspiring devotional for those seeking to deepen their love for the Eucharist."

Rev. Eric L. Boelscher STL,
Pastor of St. Joseph Parish, Crescent Springs, Kentucky

Table of Contents

Foreword	1
Introduction	5
Chapter 1 Melchizedek, the King of Salem	9
Chapter 2 The Jewish Passover	23
Chapter 3 The Manna	39
Chapter 4 The Old Temple	55
Chapter 5 Elijah and the Hearth Cakes	71
Chapter 6 Bethlehem, The House of Bread	87
Chapter 7 The Wedding Feast at Cana	101
Chapter 8 The Multiplication of the Loaves	113
Chapter 9 The Bread of Life Discourse	127
Chapter 10 The Last Supper	139
Chapter 11 The Road to Emmaus	155
Chapter 12 The Marriage Supper of the Lamb	169
Conclusion	181

Foreword

Foreword

In a world marked by rapid change and fleeting moments, the quest for meaning and depth in our spiritual journey becomes increasingly vital. Amidst the clamor of many voices, one timeless truth remains--our Catholic faith, especially as encountered in the Blessed Sacrament. The Holy Eucharist provides a steadfast anchor in the storms of change.

In the book, guided by the biblical framework made palpable in the *"Stations of the Eucharist"* Denise Mercado offers a reflective exploration of the Eucharistic Mystery. She invites the reader to consider how the Eucharist, far from being a mere ritual, is the very source and summit of our life of faith, a transformative force that inspires hope and renewal.

The pilgrimage of the *Stations of the Eucharist* begins with the biblical figure of Melchizedek, the Old Testament High Priest, who offers bread and wine in a gesture of worship and thanksgiving. Melchizedek foreshadows Christ, revealing God's intricate plan of salvation. His offering anticipates the one and for all Sacrifice Jesus offered on the Cross.

From Melchizedek, the author leads the devout pilgrim from Old Testament foreshadowing to New Testament fulfillment and the climax in Jesus' gift of the Eucharist, as a memorial of His one Sacrifice in which Jesus offers Himself as the Priest, the Altar, and the Lamb of Sacrifice. As one proceeds through the stations, the unfolding narrative invites the reader to comprehend the richness of God's New Covenant with the human family, a covenant renewed in every Mass.

As you pray this devotion, you will find that the different chapters make the Eucharistic Mystery more comprehensible.

The *Stations of the Eucharist* will help the faithful follower of Christ reflect more deeply on the mystery of the Blessed Sacrament. The connection between the Eucharist and the Cross will become more apparent, enlightening how Christ's sacrifice imbues our worship with profound meaning. Each step in this devotional journey encourages one to reflect on the parallel between Christ's road to Calvary and the gift of Himself in Holy Communion, challenging us to receive the fullness of Christ's love and mercy poured out for us in His sacrifice, stimulating our intellect and engaging our minds.

I hope you experience a sense of awe when reflecting on the different chapters. Each station captures key moments and symbols that frame our understanding of Jesus Christ, the Bread of Life. In moments of quiet, may you be reminded of the abundance of God's love made known by Jesus upon the Cross and his gift of the Eucharist as a perpetual memorial of his dying and rising for our salvation.

As Denise Mercado's Bishop, I am pleased to encourage you to let her guide you through the stations so that you might witness God's continuous narrative through the Old and New Testament, which finds its highest expression upon the Altar. From the manna in the desert to the Last Supper, the scriptures unite in a profound tapestry illustrating God's faithfulness and desire for communion with His people.

As you embark on the journey through the Stations of

the Eucharist, may your heart be open to the workings of the Holy Spirit, leading you to greater knowledge of your faith. I pray that you will see the fullness of the Eucharistic Mystery, the heart of our faith, and the lifeblood of our relationship with Christ.

Most Reverend Gregory Parkes
Bishop of St. Petersburg

Introduction

Introduction

The history of the Catholic Church is packed with spiritual treasures. As we dig for truth, we move closer to God. This helps us to become all that He wants us to be.

The Catholic Church, established by Jesus Christ, has many rich traditions. One of these rich traditions is the **Stations of the Cross**. As noted in my book – *Mary's Life Journey & Her Amazing Yes!* – the Stations of the Cross evolved over time. The original goal was to embark on a pilgrimage to experience the actual journey of Jesus, known as the Via Dolorosa or the Way of the Cross. However, "when the Muslim Turks blocked access to the Holy Land, reproductions of the stations [the places on the Via Dolorosa] were erected at spiritual centers" and eventually became an expected fixture in every Catholic Church.[1]

While cleaning an old desk in my parish office, I found a one-page typed document on the **Stations of the Resurrection**. These are different from the Stations of the Cross and focus on the events that begin with the Resurrection to the day of Pentecost. This finding inspired me to research and write about these stations in my book *The Way of Light: The Story Behind the Stations of the Resurrection*. As I began research for my second book on the Stations of the Resurrection, I asked one of the women in my parish if she ever heard of these stations. She had never heard of the Stations of the Resurrection; however, she quickly responded with information about the **Stations of the Eucharist**. I took note of the discovery. Once my book on the Stations of the Resurrection was complete, I knew I wanted to look further into the Stations of the Eucharist.

The Stations of the Eucharist begin with the Old Testament story of Melchizedek, King of Salem, and continue to the Marriage Supper of the Lamb. The purpose of these stations is to help believers deepen their understanding and appreciation of the Eucharist, which, as the *Catechism of the Catholic Church* states, is *the source and summit of our faith* (CCC 1324). This devotion is rooted in scripture both from the Old and New Testaments. Further research for this book uncovered the connection between the **Stations of the Cross** and the **Stations of the Eucharist**. Throughout the chapters in this book, we will explore this connection.

The Poor Clares of Perpetual Adoration in Hanceville, Alabama – formerly led by EWTN (Eternal World Television Network) founder Mother Angelica, are strong promoters of this devotion.[2] I had the opportunity to visit the Shrine of the Blessed Sacrament in Hanceville, Alabama. This beautiful complex includes the main church and monastery for the Sisters of the Poor Clares, as well as several other European-style structures.[3] Behind the Castle of San Miguel, which houses the Gift Shop of El Niño, is an outdoor garden that displays the twelve Stations of the Eucharist. As you enter the garden, you are led by a walkway to each of the stations displayed by a picture and an explanation for each. My journey through this beautiful garden was a peaceful reflection of what God has done for us in the Eucharist. It is my goal to share this experience with you.

The God we serve is a God of great details. There are so many connections from the Old and New Testaments that point us to the presence of Jesus – Body, Blood, Soul, and Divinity – in the Eucharist. This is truly the Blessed Sacrament. Join me as we walk through each station and learn the many details God has prepared for our instruction.

Chapter 1

Melchizedek, the King of Salem

Chapter 1

Melchizedek, The King of Salem

In the Book of Genesis, we are told of the parting of Abram and his nephew Lot. Due to quarrels between the herdsmen of Abram's livestock and the herdsmen of Lot's livestock, Abram thought it best that they go their separate ways. Abram allowed Lot to choose where he would like to settle. As they looked over the lands before them, Abram told Lot, "if you prefer the left, I will go to the right; if you prefer the right, I will go to the left."[4] Lot chose the better portion of land that was "abundantly watered" and looked "like the Lord's own garden, or like Egypt."[5] This land was the Jordan Plain. Lot pitched his tents near Sodom. The inhabitants of Sodom, however, were "wicked and great sinners against the Lord."[6]

Abram, as promised, went in the opposite direction, and settled in the land of Canaan. God then spoke to Abram and told him that "all the land that you see I will give to you and your descendants forever. I will make your descendants like the dust of the earth; if anyone could count the dust of the earth, your descendants too might be counted."[7] God then instructed Abram to walk the land and see it for himself. Abram then moved his tent and settled at Hebron where he built an altar to the Lord.[8]

Scripture does not tell us if Lot thanked the Lord in any way. Lot made his choice based on physical attraction. I wonder if he knew that Sodom was part of the land that he chose and of the wickedness that existed there.

The story continued with a war that involved "four kings against five."[9] The land mass in this war extended throughout a large region and included the city of Sodom, where Lot lived. In this war, the King of Sodom was defeated, and Lot was taken captive along with all his possessions. One of the survivors of the siege in Sodom notified Abram of his nephew's plight. Abram organized 318 armed soldiers to rescue Lot. Abram was successful in recovering his nephew along with all his possessions. When Abram returned victorious, the King of Sodom "went out to greet him in the Valley of Shaveh (that is the King's Valley).[10]

As this war began, several kings were mentioned in Scripture. However, the first time the King of Salem was mentioned was when Abram arrived victorious in the Valley of Shaveh, also known as the King's Valley. Melchizedek was the King of Salem, and he brought to Abram bread and wine. This was a precursor to the Eucharist. He also provided a blessing on Abram by "God Most High."[11] This interaction between Abram and Melchizedek occurred before Abram's name was changed to Abraham. This name change occurred once the covenant was established between God and Abram and before the Lord visited Abram by the oak of Mamre.[12]

So, who was Melchizedek, and what, if anything, was significant about his ruling city, Salem? Melchizedek was mentioned in three books of the Bible. The first mention was in the Book of Genesis, as noted above. Reference was also made in Psalms 110 as well as in the New Testament letter to the Hebrews. Melchizedek was ruler over the city of Salem, which means *shalom* or *cosmic, harmonious peace*, and his name means *king of righteousness*.[13] In addition, several other resources, including the *Catechism of the Catholic Church*, shed light on the mysterious priest of the Old Testament named Melchizedek.

Psalm 110 was an important Messianic psalm and began with a declaration: "The Lord says to my lord: 'Sit at my right hand, while I make your enemies your footstool.'"[14] Pope Benedict summed up Psalm 110 as an invitation to look at Jesus Christ to "understand the meaning of true kingship, which is to be lived as service and the giving of self, following a path of obedience and love 'to the end.'" According to Pope Benedict, when we pray this psalm, we "ask the Lord to enable us to proceed along this same journey, following Christ, the Messiah, willing to ascend with Him on the hill of the cross to accompany Him in glory, and to look to Him seated at the right hand of the Father, the victorious king and merciful priest Who gives forgiveness and salvation to all mankind."[15]

Saint Robert Bellarmine, an Italian Jesuit and Doctor of the Catholic Church, shed light on Psalm 110 with a focus on who the Lord God was speaking to in the first verse of the psalm. According to Saint Bellarmine, God was speaking to Christ, "for it cannot apply to Abraham or Ezechias, as some of the Jews will have it, neither of whom sat on the right hand of the Father, nor were they begot from the womb before the day-star, nor were they priests according to the order of Melchizedek." Saint Bellarmine also stated that "when the passage was quoted by Christ when arguing with the Jews, they did not attempt to question its reference to the Messiah."[16] In the Gospel of Matthew, Jesus asked the Pharisees, "What is your opinion about the Messiah? Whose son is he?" The Pharisees replied that the Messiah was David's son. David was the author of Psalm 110. Jesus then said to them, "How, then, does David, inspired by the Spirit, call him 'lord.'" Jesus continued, "If David calls him 'lord,' how can he be his son?" It was then clearly noted in Scripture that "no one was able to answer him a word, nor from that day on did anyone dare to ask him any more questions."[17]

The reference in Psalm 110 to the "womb before the day-star," according to Saint Bellarmine, "meant the secret and intimate essence of the Deity." He continued, "Though the womb is to be found in woman only, still it is applied to the Father, to show more clearly the consubstantiality of the Son with Him, as also to show that God needed not the cooperation of woman to bring forth and produce."[18]

In addition, Saint Bellarmine's explanation brought further clarity to the psalm. Saint Bellarmine stated that "Melchizedek succeeded no priest, nor had he a successor." It was also noted that "Melchizedek was both king and priest." Aaron, the brother of Moses, is an important Levite priest in the Old Testament.[19] Saint Bellarmine provided a comparison and noted that although Aaron was a priest, it was Melchizedek who maintained the role of both priest and king. Saint Bellarmine stated that "Melchizedek's offering consisted of bread and wine. The offering of Aaron consisted of sheep and oxen. Melchizedek was the priest of mankind; Aaron's priesthood was confined to the Jews. Melchizedek required neither tent, tabernacle, nor temple for sacrifice, Aaron did."[20]

Saint Bellarmine continued his explanation and stated that Christ is "a priest according to the order of Melchizedek by reason of having succeeded no priest and by reason of his having had no priest to succeed him." His explanation continued in that Christ's "human nature has really no father, and as to his divine nature has no mother." "The same Christ," he continued, "is both King and Priest, and he offered bread and wine at his last supper, that is, his body under the appearance of bread, and his blood under the appearance of wine; and he is the priest, not only of the Jews, but of the Gentiles."[21]

In the same way, an article by *Catholic Straight Answers* stated that Saint Paul, in the Letter to the Hebrews, "compares and contrasts the priesthood of Melchizedek with that of Aaron, the Levitical Priesthood" and notes that "Melchizedek has no genealogy in the Old Testament." Therefore, the priesthood of Melchizedek "is not based on heredity." The article continued that "Christ, like Melchizedek, is a priest by divine appointment, and His priesthood does not depend upon hereditary ties." The article further showed that because of this realization, it was noted that the "Levitical Priesthood would be replaced by the greater, perfect, and royal priesthood of Christ."[22]

The Catechism of the Catholic Church also provides information on the identity of Melchizedek and his relationship to Christ. In Section 58 of the *Catechism*, it stated, "The Bible venerates several great figures among the Gentiles. Examples given are Abel, the just, Noah, Daniel, Job, and the king-priest Melchizedek."[23] The Church, as stated in the *Catechism*, "sees in the gesture of the king-priest Melchizedek, who 'brought out bread and wine,' a prefiguring of her own offering."[24] "Everything that the priesthood of the Old Covenant prefigured," as noted in the *Catechism*, "finds its fulfillment in Christ Jesus, the 'one mediator between God and men.' The Christian tradition considered Melchizedek, 'priest of God Most High,' as a prefiguration of the priesthood of Christ, the unique 'high priest after the order of Melchizedek...'"[25]

In addition, many Christians have also believed that Melchizedek was a pre-incarnate appearance of Christ.[26] However, "Melchizedek is not Jesus. He is a representation or prefiguring of Jesus." This was confirmed in Psalm 110 and in the letter to the

Hebrews. The name Melchizedek, as noted earlier, was a title that means "king of righteousness."[27] Melchizedek is also known as a "pagan priest who recognizes the one supreme deity, using the title, 'God Most High,' just as the Jewish people would."[28]

There were also various traditions as to the identity of Melchizedek. "Hebrew tradition states that Melchizedek was Shem or a son of Shem," who was "the son of Noah." However, other traditions "stipulate that Melchizedek was a grandson of Canaan." Several resources were cited to prove each tradition, including an *Ethiopian Book of Adam and Eve*. However, according to the Jewish Encyclopedia, "Melchizedek appealed with especial force as a type of the monotheist of the pre-Abrahamic time or of non-Jewish race, like Enoch." "Abraham," according to the Jewish Encyclopedia, "learned the practice of charity from Melchizedek." In additional sources, we learned that Saint Justin Martyr argued "that Melchizedek was the uncircumcised high priest who blessed the circumcised Abraham."[29]

During the Catholic Mass, Eucharistic Prayer I, according to the General Instruction of the Roman Missal, may always be used.[30] This prayer is said in preparation of the bread and wine offered by the priest and the people at each Mass. The following is an excerpt from Eucharistic Prayer I:

Look with favor on these offerings and accept them as once you accepted the gifts of your servant Abel, the sacrifice of Abraham, our father in faith, and the bread and wine offered by your priest Melchizedek.[31]

Upon receiving the bread and wine from Melchizedek, Abram gave Melchizedek a "tenth of everything" that was recovered from his victory in rescuing Lot.[32]

Reflection

As I reflect on this station, I think about the exchange that took place between Melchizedek and Abram. Did Abram know Melchizedek before this encounter? I am sure he was aware that Melchizedek was the king of Salem. But did Abram ever meet Melchizedek face to face before this encounter? Perhaps this was their first meeting. Perhaps Abram recognized Melchizedek by his special clothing or crown?

In the same way, I wonder what Melchizedek heard about Abram. Did he hear about the separation between Abram and Lot and how this occurred? I am sure he knew of the wars that took place in the land of Sodom and the defeat that resulted in the capture of Lot. He may also have heard about Abram's plan to rescue Lot. Was Melchizedek concerned for Abram's safety during this rescue mission?

The scene where Melchizedek meets Abram takes place immediately following Abram's victory on the battlefield. The exchange includes Melchizedek blessing Abram by "God Most High." Melchizedek was not a pagan king. He was a king and priest who knew God. If Melchizedek knew about Abram's determination to rescue Lot, I wonder if he prayed to God for Abram's safety. I believe there was a connection between the two men. Perhaps they did not meet prior to this encounter. I believe Melchizedek heard of Abram's desire to save Lot and that he prayed for Abram's success in the mission. Melchizedek knew where the armies would assemble after the mission. Melchizedek came specifically to see Abram. His gifts to Abram were carefully selected to honor this man of God.

Melchizedek, in his role as a priest, made sacrifices to God. That is one of the many functions of the priest. The question I wrestle with is, "Why did Melchizedek bring out bread and wine?" As I researched this issue, I found an article by JP Nunez from *Catholic Exchange* that addressed this question. Although Scripture does not explicitly answer this question, according to Nunez, "it does give us a clue." Nunez points out that Scripture "suggests that the bread and wine were somehow linked to his priesthood, so he did not bring them out just because he thought Abram might have been hungry. Rather, he brought them out because he was a priest, and since priests are, by definition, people who offer sacrifice, he must have offered them to God as a sacrifice."[33]

An article by Scott Hahn sheds further light on *The Meal of Melchizedek*. Hahn states that Scripture makes a "sharp contrast between the Levitical priests who continue to offer animals in sacrifice." He states that the Levitical priests "had to sacrifice millions of sheep, millions of goats, and millions of cattle with millions of gallons of blood running down through the temple." He concludes that this was necessary "because of the golden calf, whereas before all of that, you had a father and a son and a clean priesthood that Melchizedek represents."[34]

The golden calf incident can be found in the Book of Exodus. In Exodus, we read that Moses ascended to Mount Sinai to meet with God. The Israelites are waiting for Moses. However, they become impatient and decide to create their own god. With the help of Aaron, Moses' brother, the Israelites create a golden calf and worship the false god instead of the one true God.

When Moses descends from Mount Sinai and sees the chaos and idol worship, he "stood at the gate of the camp and shouts, 'Whoever is for the Lord, come to me!'" The Levites come forward, and after a harrowing incident involving the slaughter of three thousand Israelites, the Levites are "installed as priests for the Lord."[35]

In Psalms 110, verse 4, we read that the "Lord has sworn and will not change his mind" and declares in the Psalm that "You are a priest forever *after the order of Melchizedek.*" The phrase, *after the order of Melchizedek,* according to Hahn, means "after the manner of Melchizedek's priesthood." This phrase suggests that "Melchizedek's manner of priestly sacrifice was bread and wine." There is no need for Melchizedek to sacrifice animals because he was a priest prior to the golden calf incident. Hahn further states that "this is how all the earthly Fathers understood this."[36]

As I continue to contemplate the encounter between Melchizedek and Abram, I envision the moment they make eye contact as they intently look into each other's eyes. Melchizedek is holding his gifts. These are special gifts, and Abram recognizes them as such. Before Abram can speak, Melchizedek brings the gifts to Abram and places them in his hands. Abram looks intently at the bread and wine and then back to the eyes of this priestly king. Abram is touched beyond words and recognizes the priestly role of Melchizedek. He understands in his heart that Melchizedek is a type of kindred spirit, a man of God. Because Abram has experienced the giving and receiving principle in his relationship with God, and because he recognizes Melchizedek as a priest of the one true God, Abram wants to give back to Melchizedek. Abram has just returned from a victorious battle. Because of the victory, he has attained many treasures. Within moments, Abram knows what he is to do. He turns to his soldiers and gives the order that a tenth of all that has been won in the battle will go to Melchizedek. Upon hearing this, I can see Melchizedek's posture straighten and a smile of gratitude appear on his face.

I have always been intrigued by the name Melchizedek. I've heard this name many times in the Mass and at Bible studies. However, it was not until this writing that I took the time to dig into the role of Melchizedek and how it relates to New Testament believers.

Melchizedek, the King of Salem is the first of Twelve Stations of the Eucharist. I encourage each of you to take the time to prayerfully meditate and contemplate on this station. Place yourself in the scene presented by the station. Are you one of Abram's soldiers witnessing this exchange between Abram and Melchizedek, or are you a servant of Melchizedek who travels with him to present the gifts of bread and wine to Abram? You could also place yourself in this scene as one of the main characters. Are you Abram returning from a victory on the battlefield? You are happy to have your nephew back safe and sound. You are proud of your soldiers, and the victory attained. Suddenly, you see the priest-king, Melchizedek. What are your first thoughts as you make eye contact? What do you think of the gifts that he is offering? Do you see a connection between the gifts presented by Melchizedek and the Eucharist we receive at each Mass?

Another main character in this station is Melchizedek. Place yourself in his shoes. What is it like to prepare the bread and wine for the journey to meet Abram? What are you thinking as you travel to meet Abram? You present the gifts to Abram, and you step back, knowing that you are doing the right thing. Suddenly, Abram gives you a tenth of all that he obtained from his victory. How does this make you feel? Do you experience a special bond with Abram because of this encounter?

Melchizedek is the beginning of this journey through the Stations of the Eucharist. Let us continue learning about the Eucharist, which is "the source and summit of our Christian life."[37]

PRAYER NOTES

PRAYER NOTES

Chapter 2

The Jewish Passover

Chapter 2

The Jewish Passover

The movie, *The Ten Commandments*, starring Charlton Heston as Moses and Yul Brynner as Rameses II, was a classic that aired around Easter every year during my childhood. This 1956 film presents the biblical story of the life of Moses and the exodus of the Jewish people from the bondage of Egyptian rule. This biblical story begins in the Book of Exodus.[38]

Through the ingenuity of Moses' mother and sister, Moses, as an infant, was found in a basket on the banks of the Nile by Pharaoh's daughter. This scheme was planned to save the child's life from Pharoah's order to kill all Jewish newborn male children. Moses was a Jew; however, because of his mother's plan, he was raised in the Egyptian palace as the grandson of the Pharaoh. As an adult, Moses witnessed the forced labor of the Jews and the injustices imposed on them. While defending a Jew from wrongdoing, Moses killed an Egyptian and tried to hide the incident. However, Pharaoh learned of the killing, resulting in Moses' exile to the land of Midian. In this foreign land, Moses married a woman named Zipporah, the daughter of Jethro. Zipporah and Moses have a son named Gershom.

After a long period of time, Pharaoh died, and the Jewish people began to cry out to God about their captivity. In the meantime, Moses came upon the mountain of Horeb, where he experienced the presence of God in the burning bush. During that experience, God commissioned Moses to rescue the Jewish people from the bondage imposed on them by the Egyptians. Although Moses hesitated to accept this role, he eventually submitted to the will of God and returned to Egypt, where he was welcomed by his brother, Aaron.

Together, both Moses and Aaron explained to the Jewish people God's plan to deliver them from the Egyptians. Moses then spoke to Pharaoh several times, making the firm request as instructed by God. "Thus says the Lord, the God of Israel: Let my people go, that they may hold a feast for me in the wilderness."[39] The stubbornness of Pharaoh was resolute. Despite the numerous plagues inflicted on the Egyptians that included gnats, flies, boils, hail, locusts, and complete darkness, Pharaoh refused to comply with God's request to "let my people go."

The Lord then said to Moses, "One more plague I will bring upon Pharaoh and upon Egypt. After that, he will let you depart."[40] Moses then presented to Pharaoh the following words from the Lord:

> *Thus says the Lord: About midnight, I will go forth through Egypt. Every firstborn in the land of Egypt will die, from the firstborn of Pharaoh who sits on his throne to the firstborn of the slave-girl who is at the handmill, as well as all the firstborn of the animals. Then there will be loud wailing throughout the land of Egypt, such as has never been or will ever be again. But among all the Israelites, among human beings and animals alike, not even a dog will growl, so that you may know that the Lord distinguishes between Egypt and Israel.* **Exodus 11:4-7**

The tenth and final plague imposed by God on the Egyptian people leads to the Second Station of the Eucharist – *the Jewish Passover*. This station is beautifully depicted in the movie *The Ten Commandments*. Beginning in Chapter 12 of the Book of Exodus, the Lord, through Moses, provided instructions to the Jewish people on what must be done to avoid the outcome of the final plague.

> *On the tenth of this month every family must procure for itself a lamb, one apiece for each household. If a household is too small for a lamb, it along with its nearest neighbor will procure one...Your lamb must be a year-old male and without blemish. You may take it from either the sheep or the goats...it will be slaughtered during the evening twilight. They will take some of its blood and apply it to the two doorposts and the lintel of the houses in which they eat it. They will consume its meat that same night, eating it roasted with unleavened bread and bitter herbs...You must not keep any of it beyond the morning; whatever is left over in the morning must be burned up...you will eat it with your loins girt, sandals on your feet and your staff in hand, you will eat it in a hurry...for you the blood will mark the houses where you are. Seeing the blood, I will pass over you; thereby, when I strike the land of Egypt, no destructive blow will come upon you.* **Exodus 12:3-13**

As we read the Jewish Passover with a New Testament understanding, truth unfolded as it related to the Eucharist.

In the Gospel of John, it was John the Baptist who referred to Jesus as the Lamb of God.[41] This was the first time in the Gospels that this occurred. In this instance, John was putting into words what he experienced in the womb of his mother, Elizabeth, when the Blessed Mother visited her while pregnant to Jesus.[42] In his mother's womb, John leaped for joy at the presence of Jesus. In the wilderness, as John provided testimony to the light of Christ, Jesus came toward him. It was at this encounter that John proclaimed, "Behold the Lamb of God, who takes away the sin of the world."[43]

In the Book of Exodus, each family was instructed to "procure for itself a lamb."[44] The *Merriam-Webster* definition of the word *procure* is *to get possession of (something); to obtain (something) by particular care and effort.*[45] As New Testament believers, we procured the Lamb of God by accepting and believing all that Jesus teaches. When Jesus instituted the Sacrament of the Eucharist at the Last Supper, we believe and, thereby, procure for ourselves the Lamb of God.

After procuring the lamb in the Old Testament, the instructions included the slaughtering of the animal. The instructions were specific and stated that the family was to "keep it (the lamb) until the fourteenth day of this month, and then, with the whole community of Israel assembled, it will be slaughtered during the evening twilight."[46] It is interesting to note that the lamb spent time with the family before it was slaughtered. Jesus spent three years ministering to the people in his time before His Passion took place. Condemnation, mockery, scourging, crowning with thorns, carrying of the cross, and the crucifixion portray the slaughter of the Lamb of God.

It is also important to note that the sacrifice of the lamb in the first Passover was fulfilled by the "father of each household." Brant Pitre, in his book, *Jesus and the Jewish Roots of the Eucharist*, stated that "no one but a priest can offer a blood sacrifice." He also noted that "at the time of the Exodus from Egypt, the priestly right of offering sacrifice belonged to all twelve tribes of Israel." Pitre also pointed out that "at the time of the exodus, there existed in Israel what might be called the 'natural priesthood' of fathers and sons, so that 'every man' would act as priest over his own household by both selecting and sacrificing the Passover lamb."[47]

Blood was a very important part of the sacrifice. In preparation for the first Passover, the families were instructed to apply the blood "to the two doorposts and the lintel of the houses in which they eat it (the lamb)."[48] Later in the Book of Exodus, we read that Moses "splashed it (the blood) on the people, saying, 'This is the blood of the covenant which the Lord has made with you...'"[49] In the Gospel of John, Jesus referred to His blood as "true drink."[50] No longer will blood be applied to an object or splashed upon us. Jesus instructed that His blood was to be consumed. He reiterated this fact at the Last Supper when He took the cup of wine and said to the apostles, "Drink from it all of you, for this is my blood of the covenant, which will be shed on behalf of many for the forgiveness of sins."[51]

As we look at the crucifixion, Jesus was already dead on the cross when a soldier thrust his lance into His side. Immediately, blood and water flowed from this wound.[52] According to the Prayer of Divine Mercy noted in the diary of Saint Faustina, the blood and water that flowed from this wound is a "fountain of mercy for us."[53] Mercy was provided to all those who put the blood of the lamb on the doorposts during the first Passover. Mercy is also shown to us as we place His blood on the doorposts of our hearts.

Once the home was secured with the blood of the lamb on the doorposts, the Jews were instructed to eat the roasted lamb "with unleavened bread and bitter herbs." We consume the Eucharist, which is the Lamb of God in the same way the Jewish people were instructed on the night of the Passover meal. The purpose of the journey for the Jewish people was to obtain freedom from Egyptian rule. Their goal was to reach the Promised Land. The lamb they consumed provided nourishment for this journey. We must recognize that as New Testament believers, our journey is similar. The purpose of our journey is to obtain freedom from ourselves, our egos, and to overcome our human failures. The Eucharist, the Lamb of God, provides nourishment for this life journey. We consume the Eucharist at each Mass and then we are sent. We are to partake of the Eucharist with an attitude of readiness to share Jesus with others in our words and actions.

In the Gospel of Matthew, Jesus clearly stated that He has come not to abolish the law but to fulfill it. He further stated that "until heaven and earth pass away, not the smallest letter or the smallest part of a letter will pass from the law, until all things have taken place."[54] The *Catechism of the Catholic Church* states that "by celebrating the Last Supper with his apostles in the course of the Passover meal, Jesus gave the Jewish Passover its definitive meaning." The death and resurrection of Jesus is the New Passover as stated in the *Catechism*. Jesus is the Lamb of God who is sacrificed for us. He is the ultimate sacrifice. This new Passover, as noted in the *Catechism,* is "anticipated in the Last Supper and celebrated in the Eucharist, which fulfills the Jewish Passover and anticipates the final Passover of the Church in the glory of the kingdom."[55]

Reflection

As I meditate on this second Station of the Eucharist, I am reminded of the challenge given to us by Saint Ignatius of Loyola in the Spiritual Exercises. In these exercises, Saint Ignatius asks us to place ourselves in the scene to better understand what God is teaching us. In accepting this challenge, I envision a typical Jewish family consisting of a father, a mother, and three children. I am the oldest son in this family. We are a close family and follow Jewish law in all things. It has been a difficult time in Egypt. My father has worked long hours making bricks for Pharaoh. I am also learning this process since I will soon be of age to work the brick lines with my father.

One evening, shortly after my father arrives home from a long day of work, we hear a call that summoned us to a meeting with Moses and Aaron. We leave our homes and follow our neighbors to the meeting place. There, Moses gives specific instructions on what each family was to do beginning "on the tenth day of the month." The details are very specific. I look at my father's face and can see that he is listening intently to all that Moses is instructing. The instructions include obtaining a lamb or goat and sprinkling the blood of the animal on our doorposts. Only after the instructions are given does Moses explain why this needs to be done. "It is the Lord's Passover," he says. "For on this same night, I [the Lord] will go through Egypt, striking down every firstborn in the land, human being and beast alike, and executing judgment on all the gods of Egypt..."[56] My eyes widen with fear as I hear these words. I am the firstborn in my family. I can feel my father's arm securely around my shoulders. As these words are spoken, I feel my father pull me close to him. Moses then continues, "But for you the blood will mark the houses where you are. Seeing the blood, I will pass over you; thereby, when I strike the land of Egypt, no destructive blow will come upon you." Shortly after these words are spoken, the meeting is over, and we are sent back to our homes. We walk in haste, thinking about the instructions given.

On the tenth of the month as instructed, my father and I go to a farm near our home to purchase a one-year-old male sheep. We find the perfect specimen and secure the creature in a special crate. As we walk home, my eyes glance several times at the crate and the lamb sitting quietly in its cage. Is this animal really going to save my life? When we arrive home, my father designates a small area off the kitchen for the lamb. Normally, the animals are kept outside. But this lamb is special according to the instructions provided by Moses. To ensure the lamb stays within the area near the kitchen, my father creates a small gate. After the animal is secured, my siblings walk toward the gated area. They place their hands over the gate and pet the animal with great care. Suddenly, my mother redirects my siblings to a variety of chores that need to be done to prepare for dinner. As I peer at this beautiful creature, I am not convinced that he will be successful in saving my life. It is at that moment that I realized that my life is not the only life in danger. Both my mother and my father are firstborns in their families. If the God of Abraham plans to strike down all the firstborn, then my parents are included in this. This lamb is very important not only to save me but that of the two most important people in my life.

After dinner, I ask my father if I can sleep in the kitchen area so that I can be close to the sheep. He looks at me with a puzzled expression but then gives his permission. As I bed down for the evening, I stare intently at the sheep. I pray to the God of Abraham that this plan would be effective and save me and my parents.

It was a chilly evening. I wrap myself in a small blanket and watch the sheep rest his head on the hay my father placed in the gated area. I can feel the heaviness of my eyes as I drift into a sound sleep. When I awake in the early morning hours, I am refreshed and very warm all over. As I move my hand toward the blanket, I feel the warmth of wool. It startles me to feel this. As I sit up, I notice that the sheep is curled up next to me and sleeping soundly. I then glance over at the gated area. The gate is open. It was secured when I went to sleep. Somehow, this lamb opened the gate and came to rest near me. At that moment, the lamb opens its eyes and immediately stands up. He shakes his body, looks around, and then moves his nose close to my face. He is a beautiful lamb. I cannot help but reach out and rub his head and ears. With that affection, I notice the lamb wag its tail with great joy. I then remember the purpose of the lamb and know that getting attached to this creature will make it difficult to follow the instructions given by Moses. With this realization, I come to my feet and quickly take the lamb to the designated area and secure the gate.

After a few days, the time has come to slaughter the lamb. My father's friend, Benjamin, and his wife, Hannah, come to our home in the early afternoon hours. Benjamin is a close friend of my father's and a newlywed. I remember attending their wedding the year prior. Hannah is now pregnant with their first child. When Moses gave the instructions from the Lord, he stated that "if a household is too small for a lamb, it along with its nearest neighbor will procure one..."[57] Because of this, my father has invited Benjamin and Hannah to join our family for this special dinner. As I gaze intently at Hannah's pregnant stomach, I wonder if the death of the firstborns would include those still in the womb. I then peer at the beautiful lamb in the gated area of our home. There are so many lives depending on this little lamb. Will this really work as God said it will?

I have never witnessed the slaughter of an animal. I am surprised that my father allows me to participate in this event. My father takes the lamb in his arms. Benjamin and I follow him to the outside covered area behind our home. Hannah joins my mother and my siblings in preparing the kitchen for the evening meal. As we exit the home, I notice my friend, Daniel, and his father as they leave the back door of their home. Daniel's father is carrying their lamb and, like my father, has a very serious look on his face. I wave to my friend before losing sight of him behind their shed.

Although my father is an expert in preparing an animal for roasting, this is different. I can see the attentiveness on his face as he moves methodically to ensure he follows all the instructions provided by Moses. It is very important that not a bone in the lamb's body is broken. It is also important to capture the blood so that it can be placed on the doorposts and lintels as instructed. Because my focus is on my father and the lamb, I did not notice as we left our home that Benjamin is carrying a large basin. My father motions to Benjamin to place the basin under one of the large hooks on the covered area of the porch. Carefully, my father slits the lamb's throat. He then hangs the lamb upside down on the hook by a very strong tendon on the back side of the leg. The blood flows quickly to the basin below. Tears well up in my eyes as I stand in front of our lamb, watching the blood flow into the basin. I did my best not to get attached to this creature. But I cannot help but recall the warmth of his beautiful wool. Although I understand the importance of the lamb as it relates to the instructions given by Moses, I am not completely convinced that this plan will work. I certainly pray for its success. After all, my life depends on it. But it is such an odd plan. How can blood on a doorpost stop death from entering?

Once the basin is full, Benjamin places it on a table in the outdoor area. My father then proceeds to prepare the lamb for cooking. When the process is complete, my father takes the lamb off the hook and, holding it in his arms, walks inside our home toward the kitchen. I follow my father as Benjamin moves slowly behind me with the basin of blood. As my mother and Hannah prepare the lamb for roasting, my father and Benjamin complete the instructions given by Moses and apply the blood to the two doorposts and the lintel. As they finish, I notice that there was blood left over. If this is going to work, I thought, maybe we should do the same to the windows and maybe even other parts of the house. It certainly wouldn't hurt. I am getting nervous about this last plague. If this does not work, not only will I die, but my siblings will be orphaned, not to mention how this will impact Hannah and her unborn child.

My mother serves the lamb with unleavened bread and herbs as Moses instructed. My father and Benjamin eat the lamb with their staff in hand, also as instructed. This is all very odd. We eat and we wait for what will happen next. Suddenly, we hear the screams and cries of men and women. We know what these cries mean. The plague of death has arrived as God had said. I hold my mother's hand tightly as the cries continue all around us. Before long, the loud wailing decreases to somber, deep cries of grief that can barely be heard. At that moment, I realize that God's plan has worked. We are safe. Death has passed over us as God said it would.

++++++++++

Sometimes, God asks us to do things that, in our minds, seem so ridiculous. However, it is not our job to question God. When we are obedient to His word, we see the greatness of God presenting Himself in our lives. Prayerfully consider this Station of the Eucharist, especially as it relates to Jesus, the Lamb of God. Is it possible for us to consume God? How does this Eucharistic meal of Jesus' Body, Blood, Soul, and Divinity, suffice for our journey through life to eternity?

PRAYER NOTES

PRAYER NOTES

Chapter 3

The Manna

Chapter 3

The Manna

It was only through God's intervention that the Israelites were freed from Egyptian bondage. The miracle of the first Passover was fresh in the minds of every Jew as they left Egypt for the Promised Land. Moses was their leader, and they were grateful for the way God was working in his life. The long journey of life, however, was filled with many ups and downs. There was a forty-year span from the time the Israelites left Egypt and entered the Promised Land. Forty years was a long time to be in transit without any roots. We all long to establish ourselves in one location. However, this was not what God had planned for the Israelites. The journey to the Promised Land would be long, with many opportunities to listen, learn, and purge within their hearts the human frailties inherited from the sin of our first parents.

Shortly after leaving Egypt, the Israelites came upon the *Wilderness of Sin*. This is an interesting name. The word *Sin* in this title, however, does not refer to the moral concept of *sin*. The name comes from the Hebrew word *Sin,* which was the Hebrew name for a particular region.[58] The Wilderness of Sin was one of six wildernesses through which the Israelites traveled on their way to Canaan. The other wildernesses were named Shur, Etham, Sinai, Paran, and Zin.[59] The Israelites arrived at the Wilderness of Sin "on the fifteenth day of the second month after their departure from the land of Egypt."[60] They had been traveling for a long time with all their belongings. Perhaps they were tired and frustrated, wondering how long it would take to get to the Promised Land.

Upon reaching the Wilderness of Sin, the Israelites grumbled against Moses and Aaron and said, "If only we had died at the Lord's hand in the land of Egypt, as we sat by our kettles of meat and ate our fill of bread!"[61] Somehow, they seemed to have forgotten about the last plague of death that ensued on all of Egypt and the protection provided by the blood of the lamb. For some reason, they were focused solely on the lack of food in the wilderness. However, they were not completely without food. The Israelites left Egypt with their herds, which furnished them with milk and meat. The provisions they took for their journey also included oil and flour.[62] I am sure by this point, any of the fruits and vegetables they took from Egypt were consumed. With provisions decreasing quickly, the Israelites worried about the makeup of each meal. Soon, they experienced hunger. In this state, they easily recalled the plentiful food available in Egypt.

Hunger is an amazing thing. Coupled with exhaustion, it was understandable how they could easily forget the miracles of freedom. The Israelites made their needs known to both Moses and Aaron. In doing so, God heard the cries of His people and said to Moses, "I am going to rain down bread from heaven..."[63] As with the Passover meal, God provided specific instructions regarding this special bread from heaven. In addition, God instructed Moses to tell the Israelites, "In the evening twilight, you will eat meat, and in the morning, you will have your fill of bread, and then you will know that I, the Lord, am your God."[64]

As stated earlier, the bread from heaven had special instructions. But before the bread appeared, the meat promised by God, in the form of quail, came in the evening hours. Quail is a small, brown-feathered bird that resembles a partridge and is well-known for its delicious meat.[65] The provision of quail was mentioned in the Old Testament in both the Book of Exodus and again in the Book of Numbers. Rabbi Joseph Kara provided an explanation for the quail narratives. In his opinion, the quail came down "only for a limited period, ceasing during the first year of the Israelites' sojourn in the wilderness." Another explanation provided by Moses Nahmanides stated that the provision of "quail was periodic" and "inconsistent" which explained how "the people in Numbers could have an unfulfilled craving for meat." Nahmanides also noted that the special bread from heaven was the "source of their subsistence" and always available.[66]

The special bread from heaven, as promised by God, appeared in the morning in a "layer of dew" and was available each day of the 40-year journey. "When the layer of dew evaporated, fine flakes were on the surface of the wilderness."[67] Not knowing what this substance was, the Israelites asked plainly, "What is it?"[68] The Hebrew word translated *manna* literally means *What is it?*[69]

The special God-given instructions regarding the manna included gathering "an *omer* for each person for as many of you as there are, each of you providing for those in your own tent."[70] An *omer* is a dry measure of approximately two quarts.[71] In addition to gathering only what was needed, it was important that the manna was eaten on the day it was gathered. Moses warned the Israelites to follow the instructions God had given. However, many of the Israelites failed to comply with the instructions provided. When the manna was not consumed on the day it was gathered, "it became wormy and stank."[72] It was also noted that on the sixth day, they were instructed to gather twice as much manna, "two omers for each person."[73] God allowed this to honor the holy Sabbath. Only on the sixth day, when the manna was stored for the following holy day, was it fit for human consumption. Moses' instructions were clear. "Six days you will gather it, but on the seventh day, the sabbath, it will not be there."[74]

Despite the specific instructions, on the Sabbath, many people went to the fields looking for manna. The Sabbath is a day given to us by God. It is a day of rest. For this reason, God instructed the people to gather a double portion of manna on the sixth day so that the people could rest on the seventh day. God's plans are always the best plans. It is not necessary for humanity to alter God's plans. Yet, so many times, our reasoning causes us to do just that.

Perhaps in a moment of concern for humanity, the Lord said to Moses, "How long will you refuse to keep my commandments and my instructions?"[75] Notice that God does not say, "How long will *they* refuse to keep my commandments..." Moses was the leader of the people, and God wanted him to lead. As a leader, Moses was responsible for all that occurred. This, perhaps, was an opportunity for Moses to sharpen his leadership skills and to help people understand the importance of God's instructions.

An article by Angie O'Gorman in the *National Catholic Reporter* addressed self-sufficiency and how this attribute is not necessarily what God was after.[76] "Had God let them be self-sufficient, they might have found their own food, or eaten less..." However, O'Gorman indicated that the specific God-given instructions helped organize the people. "They had to figure out a way to collect and distribute and consume this daily edible event..."

Merriam-Webster Dictionary defines community as a group of people living in the same place or having a particular characteristic in common.[77] Feelings of fellowship and interdependence were strengthened as members of a community interacted and worked together. The need to organize allowed the Israelites to effectively conform to the God-given instructions. As a result, community was established "with all its riches and limits, its brokenness and grandeur, its need for rules and rituals."[78]

In addition to the need for food, there were other obstacles encountered during the 40-year journey through the desert. The sense of community, however, allowed the Israelites to disregard self-sufficiency and rely on God's promises. There may have been many Israelites who had difficulty walking under the desert sun. Some may have gotten sick while others grew old. According to O'Gorman, self-sufficiency would say: "These people can be left behind. We should be as independent from these people as possible. They impede everything. They can cost you your life."

However, as indicated in O'Gorman's article, there was no "biblical basis for leaving anyone behind." The journey was successful because the Israelites formed a community based on the promises of God and His instructions. They ignored self-sufficiency and loved one another as they formed a community with God at the center of their existence. God brought the Israelites through the desert "so as to test you by affliction, to know what was in your heart."[79] God's plans are always better than our plans. Sometimes, however, His plans are troubling. We might wonder why affliction is necessary. As we ask these questions, we must listen intently to the answer God provides. Regarding the Israelites' 40-year journey in the desert, the Old Testament provided an explanation.

> *He, therefore, let you be afflicted with hunger, and then fed you with manna, a food unknown to you*

and your ancestors, so you might know that it is not by bread alone that people live, but by all that comes forth from the mouth of the Lord.
Deuteronomy 8:3

Reflection

As I consider the challenge to place myself in this station, there are several positions to contemplate. I choose to focus on the role of a wife and mother traveling from Egypt and reacting to new rituals developed along the way. I am so grateful to God for the release from Egyptian bondage. My concern is for my two older sons, who are coming of age and being trained to work the brutal tasks imposed by the Egyptians. I have watched these harsh tasks prematurely age my husband's body and mind. Now, with God's help, we are free from Egyptian cruelty. We are on our way to the Promised Land.

My family is together, and we are happy. My husband now walks with his head held high and a smile on his face. It has been a long time since I have seen him this happy. My children bounce with joy as they walk alongside their father. My sons are learning what it is to be a man, and soon they will be ready for marriage. With the help of other women in our tribe, I have identified several prospective brides for each of my sons. My daughter is still too young to be considered for marriage. However, from an early age, she has worked with me in preparing meals and caring for the family. In God's time, I know that she will be a wonderful wife and mother.

As we prepared for this journey, my daughter and I packed all the essential kitchen items along with all the food that was available to us. My sons assisted my husband in rounding up our livestock and ensured the cart was well-equipped for the long journey. Our two donkeys were harnessed to the cart that stored all our belongings. My husband and I take turns driving the cart as we travel farther and farther away from Egypt.

The caravan stops periodically so we can prepare meals for our family. The first several stops are quite enjoyable as my daughter and I prepare food for my husband and my sons. This feeling of peace is short-lived as we traverse farther and farther into the desert. As our food supply diminishes, my concern heightens. Several women from other families share their concerns as well. We share food among ourselves and wonder what God has in store for us. My husband and I discuss our concerns every evening after each meal. In addition to food concerns, the new surroundings are a challenge. This is a desert. At times, it is difficult for the donkeys to pull the cart through the desert sand. The heat during the day is quite exhausting, which brings concern for our water supply. I am beginning to be afraid of this adventure, not knowing where it would lead. I did not want my family to die in bondage in Egypt. Now, I am concerned that they will die in the desert. Before long, the people speak out harshly to both Moses and Aaron about their concerns. I cringe when I hear one of the rabbis raise his voice to Moses. The fear of the people is real and justified. Where will we get food to eat in this barren place? How much longer can we go on without food?

My quiet time with the Lord has always been in the morning hours. I rise early in the morning before the rest of the family to prepare the first meal of the day. Before doing so, I spend time with the Lord in prayer. It is during these times that I am reminded of the miracles that God provided not only for my family but for all the Israelites. We were protected by the blood of the lamb during the last plague that convinced

Pharaoh to allow us to leave Egypt. However, the miracle that remains so entrenched in my mind is the parting of the sea. Several days after leaving Egypt, Pharaoh became very angry and decided to attack us. "Pharaoh harnessed his chariots and took his army with him...all Pharaoh's horses, his chariots, his horsemen, and his army", and caught up to us as we encamped by the sea.[80]

It took us a few days to arrive at the Red Sea. It is a beautiful place to set up camp before continuing the journey. However, I remember the disturbance and the fear that mounted when the men in our group announce that the Egyptians were on their way. My husband jumps on the cart to get a better view. I can see from the expression on his face that things do not look good. This is the first time I hear the men in our group complain boldly to Moses and Aaron about our situation. "What have you done to us, bringing us out of Egypt? Did we not tell you this in Egypt, we said, 'Leave us alone that we may serve the Egyptians?' Far better for us to serve the Egyptians than to die in the wilderness."[81] Although my husband and I were happy to leave Egypt, not everyone in our caravan feels the same way. However, the confidence in Moses' voice brings an assurance of safety.

> *"Do not fear!"* he boldly exclaimed. *"Stand your ground and see the victory the Lord will win for you today. For these Egyptians whom you see today you will never see again. The Lord will fight for you; you have only to keep still."* **Exodus 14:13-14**

My eyebrows raise in wonder as I contemplate the command to keep still. This is not a calming situation. I close my eyes and say a quick prayer, "Lord, please help us." I open my eyes when I hear one of the children call out and direct us to a cloud that hovers between all of us and Pharoah's army. It is a different cloud formation than we have ever seen. That evening, the cloud "illumined the night"[82] so that the Egyptians could not come any closer. It is then that Moses "stretched out his hand over the sea; and the Lord drove back the sea with a strong east wind all night long and turned the sea into dry ground."[83] We enter the sea on dry land, with the water as a wall to our right and to our left. I have never seen anything like this before. It is quite scary yet peaceful. It is difficult to explain the emotions that are running through my heart as my family and I walk with our cart and all our belongings through the sea on dry land.

After all of us reach the other side, we notice the cloud that prevented the Egyptians from advancing is gone. The Egyptians come to the edge of the sea and examine the situation. I am sure that they have never seen this type of phenomenon. They look to the right and left and can see, as we did, a wall of water on each side with a clear path before them. Perhaps they recall the various plagues that tormented them and thought this was another scheme by the God of Israel. In their minds, they may have reasoned that despite the strange phenomenon of each plague, they survived all of it, except of course, their firstborn. This is the driving force behind their anger. They are determined to seek what they believe is justice for the death of their loved ones. With this vengeful determination, the Egyptians charge forward with the wall of water on either side of their chariots. This occurs in the early morning hours before dawn. I witness this during my morning prayer time. I hold my hands over my mouth as I see the chariots move quickly toward us. Suddenly, the same cloud formation appears, and with it, the Egyptian chariots seem to sink in the sand. Their difficulty brings panic as they try to force their horses to move through the sand. This difficulty forces them to turn their chariots back toward Egypt. As I watch this spectacle unfold, I notice Moses stretching out his hands toward the sea in the same way he did earlier. It is now daybreak, and the sun is coming over the horizon. As Moses raises his hands, "the water flowed back" and "covered the chariots and the horsemen. Of all Pharaoh's army which had followed the Israelites into the sea, not even one escaped."[84]

By now, my family and fellow travelers are awake. I cannot dare say what I had just seen. However, we each witness the bodies of the Egyptians "lying dead on the seashore."[85] God's great power once again has saved us. This is a miracle I know I will never forget.

Yet here we are facing another challenge. This time, our enemy lies within our stomachs as we long for food to sustain us on this journey. Moses tells us that God has heard our grumbling. He then tells us that God will provide meat in the evening and bread in the morning.[86] Of course, we have no idea how this is going to happen. Soon, it is evening, and we see over the entire camp beautiful quail. The last time I saw a quail was in Egypt. I immediately think of all the great recipes I can use to feed my family. My husband and sons gather several of the quail for our evening meal. It is such a joyful meal. We savor every mouthful.

The next morning during my prayer time, I thank God for the beautiful quail. Shortly before the sun rose, I notice the dew throughout the camp. Within a few minutes, the dew disappears, and in its place is an odd, flake-like substance I've never seen before. By this time, my husband and children are awake. We walk, along with other families, toward the substance. We are all very curious. One by one, we say, "What is it?"

Moses then provides the explanation that the flakes are the bread promised by God. He then provides specific instructions on how the flakes are to be gathered. We all listen intently. Each day, our family follows the specific instructions provided. We do not gather more than is allowed. Also, on the sixth day, we are sure to gather the double portion prescribed so that we can rest on the Sabbath. There are, however, several in our caravan who do not follow the instructions, which, in the end, angers God. I remember talking with my neighbors about following the instructions explicitly the way Moses had directed them. Eventually, every one of us did as we were told. Several women came up with different recipes that included baking or boiling. My favorite is to mix the flakes, which we call *manna*, with several spices and bake them in loaf pans that I received from my mother and grandmother many years ago.

I am grateful for the manna that appears every day during this journey. I do not know how long this journey will last. It is good to know that God is providing for us as we move through this desert. I am looking forward to entering the Promised Land with my husband and children.

++++++++++

Prayerfully consider this Station of the Eucharist as it relates to this journey of life. Do we follow the instructions God has given us? Do we accept the bread from heaven that is readily available to us? Do we acknowledge Jesus in the Eucharist – Body, Blood, Soul, and Divinity and recognize that He is the bread from heaven that sustains us through this journey of life? The *Catechism of the Catholic Church* tells us that the Eucharist is "the source and summit of our Christian life."[87] Spend time sharing with God your understanding and thankfulness for the Eucharist.

PRAYER NOTES

PRAYER NOTES

Chapter 4

The Old Temple

Chapter 4

The Old Temple

In the history of Israel, there were two temples noted. The first was built by King Solomon around 970 B.C. This temple was destroyed by the Babylonians in 586 B.C. The second temple was built after the return from the Babylonian Exile in 516 B.C. This second temple was renovated and enlarged by King Herod the Great around 19 B.C. and was destroyed by the Romans in 70 A.D. Both temples were built on the Temple Mount. The Western Wall is the only remnant of the second temple. It is the holiest site for the Jews because it is the closest spot to where the *Holy of Holies* once stood.[88]

The Old Temple, referred to in the Second Station of the Eucharist, was the first temple. The plans for the first temple were established by King David. It was David's intent to build the temple. However, the Lord spoke to David and said,

> *You have shed much blood, and you have waged great wars. You may not build a house for my name, because you shed too much blood upon the earth in my sight. However, a son will be born to you. He will be a peaceful man, and I will give him rest from all his enemies on every side. For Solomon shall be his name, and in his time, I will bestow peace and tranquility on Israel. It is he who shall build a house for my name; he shall be a son to me, and I will be a father to him, and I will establish the throne of his kingship over Israel forever.* **1 Chronicles 22:8-10**

At the beginning of his reign as king over Israel, Solomon journeyed to Gibeon and "offered sacrifice in the Lord's presence on the bronze altar at the tent of meeting" established by Moses and later his father, David.[89] On the evening the sacrifice was offered, God spoke to Solomon and told him that He would give him whatever he asked. Solomon asked only for wisdom and knowledge to govern the people. God was pleased with this request and provided Solomon with not only what he requested but also riches, treasures, and glory.[90] Shortly after receiving God's blessings, Solomon decided to build the temple. However, Solomon was determined that the temple would be a great design "for our God is greater than all other gods." Solomon questioned, "Who is really able to build him [God] a house, since the heavens and even the highest heavens cannot contain him?" He further questioned, "Who am I that I should build him a house, unless it be to offer incense in his presence?"[91] Solomon grappled with these questions during his interaction with the king of Tyre. He then hired skilled workers from the king of Tyre, who were experts in gold, silver, bronze, and iron. Solomon also solicited the support of workers skilled in purple, crimson, and violet fabrics as well as engraved work.

The king of Tyre responded to Solomon's request by sending him a "craftsman of great skill" named Huram-abi. Huram-abi assisted with the construction of the temple, especially as it related to the intricate details of design. In addition to many other skilled craftsmen, the king of Tyre also provided Solomon with lumber from Lebanon, which was transported in rafts to the port of Joppa. In return for the skilled assistance and building materials, Solomon sent to the king of Tyre wheat, barley, oil, and wine. To ensure productivity for the building of the temple, Solomon took a census of the men sent from Tyre and organized them as carriers, cutters, and overseers.[92]

The construction of the temple, according to an article by *Young Catholics*, "symbolized the dwelling place of God among His people." It was "the meeting point between the earthly realm and the divine, where God's presence could be experienced in a unique and tangible way."[93] Specific instructions were provided by Solomon regarding the construction of the temple as well as the many articles that were placed in this holy dwelling. Research by Winfried Corduan, Professor Emeritus of Philosophy and Religion at Taylor University, indicated the dimensions of the temple. According to Corduan, the "innermost sanctuary was a square 30 feet by 30 feet." The nave and the vestibule were longer than the innermost sanctuary but no wider. Only priests were allowed inside the temple for the purpose of offering sacrifices to God on behalf of the people. Gold and precious stones were used throughout the temple structure.[94]

Within the innermost sanctuary, known as the *Holy of Holies*, Solomon commissioned skilled craftsmen to carve two cherubim. These cherubim "stood upon their own feet," facing toward the nave, and were covered in gold. The wingspan of both cherubim side by side filled the space, wall to wall, in the *Holy of Holies*. The special veil in the inner sanctuary was made of violet, purple, crimson, and fine linen and had cherubim embroidered upon it.[95] Other items created for use in the temple included "the golden altar, the tables on which the showbread lay, the menorahs and their lamps of pure gold...flowers, lamps, and gold tongs...snuffers, bowls, cups, and firepans of pure gold." In addition, "the inner doors to the *Holy of Holies*, as well as the doors to the nave of the temple, were of gold."[96]

The Ark of the Covenant, which contained "the gold jar of manna, the staff of Aaron that had sprouted, and the tablets of the covenant,"[97] also known as the Ten Commandments, was placed in the *Holy of Holies* by the Levites. The Levites were a class of warrior priests who gained the role of priesthood following the slaughter of the golden calf idolaters at Mount Sinai.[98] In addition, the Levites were also singers and musicians "with cymbals, harps, and lyres." As they raised their voices and musical instruments to praise the Lord, a cloud descended upon the temple and "the glory of the Lord filled the house of God."[99]

During the dedication of the temple, Solomon recognized the presence of the Lord. In response, Solomon turned to the assembly of Israel and blessed the people. He then knelt before the people, and with outstretched hands toward heaven, Solomon prayed not only for the people of Israel but also for the foreigners, "who come from a distant land for the sake of your great name...and come in prayer to this house." Solomon asked God to "do all that the foreigner asks of you, that all the people of the earth may know your name, may revere you as do your people Israel, and may know that your name has been invoked upon this house that I have built." Although the temple was built for the benefit of the people of Israel, Solomon recognized the immense love of God for all people. He also seemed to understand the restlessness that exists in every heart and acknowledges that "there is no one who does not sin." Only God knows "the heart of every human being." Therefore, Solomon prayed that God's eyes and ears "be attentive to the prayer of this place."[100] Immediately following the prayers of Solomon, "fire came down from heaven and consumed the burnt offerings and sacrifices, and the glory of the Lord filled the house." All the people assembled "fell down upon the pavement with their faces to the earth and worshiped, praising the Lord, 'who is so good, whose love endures forever.'"[101]

Reflection

When acknowledging the greatness of God, it is only fitting that our churches are built with the best materials and with skilled laborers. As I contemplate this station, I place myself in the scene as a craftsman under the direction of Huram-abi, who was specifically assigned to this project by the king of Tyre. It is midday when Huram-abi addresses a team of workers. We are woodcarvers and have worked for several weeks on a special project for the King of Tyre. During Huram-abi's address, he shares the details of a new project that will take place in a distant land. This is an international endeavor that is commissioned by the king of Israel. In return, the king of Israel will send a variety of products to our land, such as wheat and barley, that will benefit our people. Huram-abi is looking for a team of six woodcarvers to assist in this special project. After an explanation of the project, he asks for volunteers. Although I am relatively new to the trade with only six years of experience, I am single and recognize this invitation as an opportunity to sharpen my skills and to visit a distant land. I immediately volunteer for the team. Huram-abi is pleased to add me to the roster.

I do not know much about the people of Israel. I have heard from my family and friends that their religion is different from ours. They worship only one God, who seems to be very specific in what he requires of them. It is my understanding from the explanation provided by Huram-abi that our team will assist in the building of a temple for Israel's God. I am excited about the project and the journey to a new place. After a few days of preparation, I meet my fellow workers at the designated location. Along with Huram-abi, we embark on a long journey. We arrive in Joppa aboard rafts containing the special wood needed for the project. We continue our journey by caravan to the Temple Mount in Jerusalem. Many suppliers with a variety of building supplies and other craftsmen are part of the caravan.

I do not know what to expect as we enter the city of Jerusalem. It is a fortified city with people living on both sides of its walls. As we enter the walled city, I notice a large staircase-like structure that seems to lead to the highest point of the city. My colleagues and I ascend the staircase following Huram-abi. At the top of the staircase, we meet the King of Israel, King Solomon. Huram-abi and King Solomon embrace. King Solomon is a middle-aged man of average height with a long dark beard. He holds a scepter in one hand as he speaks with Huram-abi. He is an authoritative figure who holds the respect and loyalty of all those around him. My eyes move from left to right as I take in my surroundings. People are walking about with purpose as they carry items and talk among themselves.

Before long, Huram-abi introduces us to the king. We are then led to a large table that hold the plans for the temple. King Solomon knows exactly what he wants in this project. His plans are very detailed. As he describes the drawings, I immediately notice a special area of the plans marked *Holy of Holies*. I listen intently as King Solomon provides an explanation of the plans. However, as he discusses the area marked *Holy of Holies*, his tone changes. This is, obviously, an important part of the temple and the detail provided by King Solomon is especially heightened because of its significance. One of the details described for this space is the carving of two cherubim that are to be covered in gold. The size of these cherubim is quite extensive. As I continue to stare intently at the plans for this special space, I hear Huram-abi state my name as one of the craftsmen assigned to the area marked *Holy of Holies.* I immediately stand erect and, with a puzzled look on my face, wonder why I have been chosen. For some reason, I feel drawn to this special room, but I am concerned that my level of expertise may not suffice for the task at hand. Later that day, Huram-abi introduces me to the team leader for the construction of the *Holy of Holies.* He is a well-known craftsman from Tyre with many years of experience. Suddenly, I realize that this is an opportunity to learn from the best. In doing so, I will build my reputation so that I can one day lead a team of craftsmen on a special project in our country or abroad.

Despite the small size of the room, the list of items to be built for the *Holy of Holies* is quite extensive. In addition to the two cherubim that I am assigned to create, the following items are also required: an altar covered in gold, a special veil made of fine linens, several tables with specific dimensions, and several doors that separate this room from the rest of the temple.

There are three woodcarvers, including myself, assigned to creating the two cherubim for the *Holy of Holies.* Huram-abi provides drawings of the cherubim along with specific dimensions. In my homeland of Tyre, we refer to cherubim as angels. In our religion, angels are recognized as beings of energy. As I study the drawing, I realize that the people of Israel have a different understanding of these beings. This drawing depicts the cherubim as guards. Their facial expressions indicate a determination to protect whatever else would be placed in this special room. In addition, the dimensions of these two objects are quite daunting, considering the size of the space. The cherubim are to stand side by side with a combined wingspan that fills the space from wall to wall.

Suddenly, the head woodcarver announces that the material for our project has arrived. As I follow the instructions of the head woodcarver, I wonder about the meaning of the cherubim in this project, and I am curious to learn about the other aspects of this special room. After weeks of working on this project, the faces of the cherubim are slowly coming to life. I am proud of the results thus far and, in a special way, I'm growing attached to these creatures. It is quite amazing to hold a block of wood in your hand and then to discover, after many hours of carving, the hidden beauty of the wood.

During one of our meal breaks, an Israelite comes into our workspace. I have never seen him before. He is dressed in special clothing. I am later told that he is a priest. He looks toward us as we eat our meal and politely nods. He then looks up toward the face of one of the cherubim. His eyes study the figure with delight. As he turns toward me, there is a smile on his face and tears in his eyes. He is obviously pleased with the work completed thus far. In the same way, he also examines the other items being made in the room. He places his hands on the altar near the entrance of the room. With his eyes closed, as if in prayer, he moves his hands slowly from left to right. After a while, the priest turns toward me, smiles, and leaves the room. I turn to the other workers, who simply continue to eat their meals. I am curious about this man and hope for an opportunity to see him again.

Several months later, the beauty of the two cherubim is on full display. It will take several more months to complete the project, but the drawing can now be seen in the carving provided by myself and my colleagues. By this time, the main altar is complete in design and ready for the final touches. In addition, several tables are purposely positioned in designated areas of the room. These tables are beautifully carved, designating their special purpose.

Throughout these many months, I have come to realize that the *Holy of Holies* is a special place of sacrifice. I also learn that all the priests of Israel have access to the temple, but only the high priest will have access to the *Holy of Holies*. I am curious about what will occur in the room and wonder if I will have an opportunity to learn about this different religion. Several days later, the same priest who came by months earlier enters the workspace. I am high on a ladder, carving details on the face of one of the cherubim when I see him enter the room. I am determined at this time to meet him. I immediately call down to him and descend as fast as I can on the ladder. As I gaze into his eyes, I smile and say, "my name is Jalal." I then extend my hand, hoping that he will acknowledge the greeting. The priest, with a surprised frown, stares at my extended hand and then back at my face. He refuses the handshake but says quite calmly, "my name is Eliab." After a brief exchange, it is confirmed that Eliab is a priest. He is an older man and very curious about the products being made. I ask him if he likes the cherubim. He responds with a smile and nods yes as he lifts his chin to see the cherubim's face. I then boldly ask if he can explain to me the purpose of this room. Before he can respond, my colleagues announce that it is time for a meal break. I ask the priest if he will join me. We walk to a separate part of the room away from the others. I offer to share my food with the priest, but he refuses the offer. Although I am hungry, I decide to spend the time wisely and listen to the priest as I ask questions.

I begin the conversation by asking about the cherubim. "Where I am from," I say, "we do not have statues of angels portrayed in this way." Eliab stares carefully at me as I continue my question. "The plans provided by your king were very specific," I say. Eliab smiles and nods yes. I then ask, "What is its meaning?" With precision, Eliab clearly states that the cherubim represent spirits who serve God. He then explains that these spirits guard God's throne and demonstrate His power and majesty. "This is an awfully small room for your God's throne," I say. "Why isn't this space bigger?" I ask. "The entire universe is God's throne," Eliab says. "But" he continues, "He has designated this room as a special place where He will visit His people." "All the specifications for this room," Eliab states, "including the items to be placed here, were given to us by God." "What is the purpose of this place?" I ask.

"Once a year," Eliab explains, "the high priest of Israel will enter this space and provide atonement for his sins and for all the people of Israel."

"How will he do that?" I ask. "There is a special ritual and prayers used for this purpose," Eliab explains. He continues, "in addition to the services provided by the high priest, the Ark of the Covenant will reside in this space." Eliab squints as he sees my puzzled expression and continues his explanation.

"The Ark of the Covenant," he says, "is a symbol of Israel's special relationship with God." "This Ark," he continues, "will be brought here by our priests and placed on this altar." Eliab motions to the altar in the room. He continues, "the Ark contains a jar of manna that signifies the sustenance provided by God during our desert journey to the Promised Land." Once again, Eliab responds to the confusion noted on my face. "Manna was the special bread God provided," he continues. "It was given to us daily and appeared on the fields after the morning dew as white flakes of grain." "Your God did that for your people?" I ask. "Yes," Eliab says as he nods with a smile. He then says that there are two other items in the Ark.

"The sprouted staff of Aaron is also included in the Ark," he says. "This staff is evidence of the exclusive right to the priesthood of the tribe of Levi. I am of the tribe of Levi" he proudly notes, "and, therefore, serve my people as a priest." "The third item in the Ark," he continues, "is the tablets of the covenant. These tablets contain the Ten Commandments given by God to Moses on Mount Sinai." I listen intently as Eliab provides insight on the important aspects of his religion. I do not completely understand all that he shares, but I am drawn to Eliab's peaceful demeanor and the confidence displayed in his words. Before long, it is time to resume work on the cherubim. We say our goodbyes. I watch as Eliab leaves the workspace, and I wonder if he will return before the project is completed.

After several years of detailed work, the temple is completed. Within the *Holy of Holies* stands the two cherubim. The gold covering of the cherubim seem to magnify the details created throughout the structure. I am proud of this work and learned so much during this process. A special veil made of fine linen is displayed in the space along with the golden altar where the Ark of the Covenant will be placed. In addition, several items, such as snuffers, lamps, bowls, cups, and firepans of pure gold are placed on the special tables.

In a beautiful ceremony, the temple is dedicated to the God of Israel. During the ceremony, the Ark of the Covenant is carried by the Levite priests. It is then that I notice Eliab as one of the carriers of the Ark. Although we do not make eye contact, I recognize the love and devotion that my new friend has for his God. It is truly a special moment. The Ark is carried into the temple. We cannot see the placement of the Ark on the altar. However, because I am so familiar with the details of this special room, I imagine what this beautiful Ark looks like as it is placed on the golden altar. I can also envision my new friend, Eliab, bowing in reverence before the Ark as it is placed in its designated space.

As the priests exit the temple, the beautiful praise music begins. There are trumpets, harps, cymbals, and a host of voices praising God. A cloud then descends from above the crowd and enters the temple. The cloud fills the new temple. This is a phenomenon I have never experienced before. Something wonderful is happening, yet I cannot explain the peace and joy that bubbles within my heart. As I try to understand all that is happening, King Solomon begins to address the crowds.

His words are so eloquent and the love for his people is so apparent in everything he says. Then, the king turns toward a beautiful altar in the middle of the courtyard and kneels in the presence of the whole assembly. He prays a beautiful prayer praising God and interceding for the people of Israel. He then acknowledges all of us who traveled from distant lands to assist in the building of the temple. His prayer asks that God will "do all that the foreigner asks of you, that all the peoples of the earth may know your name, may revere you as do your people Israel, and may know that your name has been invoked upon this house that I have built."[102] It is a beautiful prayer. In the stillness of the moment, only King Solomon's voice can be heard. All the people assembled, Israelites and foreigners alike, listen intently and reverently to the words spoken by the king. Immediately after his prayer, fire comes down from heaven and consumes the offerings positioned on the altar, and the glory of the Lord fills the temple in a way I have never known possible. The people respond as they immediately kneel with their faces to the earth and worship God. I join them in this special adoration and wonder if this one God could be the only God of this vast universe.

++++++++++

As you enter the beauty of a Catholic Church, spend time looking at a piece of art displayed in the church. Consider the artist who first sketched the piece and then consider the builders. As you study the art piece, think of your life. The artist and the builder in our lives is God. Like Jalal, we are curious about the things God is doing in our lives and so we ask questions. Spend time in the house of the Lord, listening to Him as He answers your questions. Consider all that occurs in your life. God is with us throughout our days. Do we hear Him?

Beyond the beauty of the sacred spaces provided in our churches, do you see yourself as a temple of the Holy Spirit? Through our baptism, we are temples where God resides. Do you have a sacred space in your home where you can spend time with God in prayer? Consider placing a piece of art in the space, such as a crucifix, a small nativity scene, or a picture of the Divine Mercy or Sacred Heart of Jesus to remind you of God's goodness and love. Spend time in your sacred space thanking God for the beautiful artwork He has created in you. This artwork is not yet complete. Spend time talking with Him about the finishing touches and the importance of the sacred space He has established in your heart and in the beautiful churches throughout the world.

PRAYER NOTES

PRAYER NOTES

Chapter 5

Elijah and the Hearth Cakes

Chapter 5

Elijah and the Hearth Cakes

The story of Elijah as it relates to the Fifth Station of the Eucharist begins in the first Book of Kings in the Old Testament. The King of Israel at the time was King Ahab, son of Omri. Ahab was the seventh king of the northern kingdom of Israel.[103] He became king in the thirty-eighth year of King Asa of Judah and reigned for twenty-two years.[104] King Ahab, as noted in Scripture, "did what was evil in the Lord's sight more than any of his predecessors."[105] He married Jezebel, daughter of the priest-king Ethbaal, ruler of the Phoenician cities of Tyre and Sidon. Under Jezebel's influence, Ahab abandoned Yahweh and established Baal and Asherah cults in Israel.[106]

Elijah was a prophet sent by God to show Israel their evil ways and to encourage them to return to the Lord. Elijah's name means *Yahweh is my God*.[107] Because of the evil in the land, Elijah spoke to King Ahab the words given to him by God.

> *As the Lord, the God of Israel, lives, whom I serve, during these years there shall be no dew or rain except at my word.* **1 Kings 17:1**

Following his announcement to King Ahab, Elijah, as instructed by God, traveled to the Wadi Cherith, east of the Jordan. While in this region, ravens brought him bread and meat. This was similar to what occurred during the Israelites' journey through the desert. During the desert journey, God provided manna and quail. In this scenario, God used the raven to provide for his servant Elijah the food he needed. In addition, Elijah had access to fresh water from the wadi. Because there was no rainfall, eventually, the wadi ran dry. When this occurred, God instructed Elijah to travel to Zarephath, where he would receive food from a widow.[108]

The story of the widow is a beautiful story of unexpected faith. The widow did not know that God was sending Elijah to her. As he arrived at the city of Zarephath, he saw the widow gathering sticks at the city's entrance. It was unlikely that she was the only one near the city's entrance. However, Elijah somehow knew that this woman was the widow that God spoke of. He called out to her and, at first, asked her for something to drink. She immediately responded and turned toward the nearby well to fulfill the request. After only two steps forward, Elijah called out to her again and asked her to also bring "a crust of bread." The woman stopped walking, turned to Elijah, and explained how she had only "a handful of flour in my jar and a little oil in my jug." She then explained, with tears in her eyes and a trembling in her voice, that her goal was to gather wood to make a fire so that she could use her last provisions to make a final meal for herself and her son. Elijah gazed into her eyes and provided words of comfort. "Do not be afraid," he told her. "Go and do as you have said." He then said, "But first, make a little cake and bring it to me. Afterward, you can prepare something for yourself and your son." This woman was standing before Elijah with a deep frown of unbelief. Perhaps in her mind, she questioned: *Who is this man who is asking so much of me?* Elijah then continued, "For the Lord, the God of Israel says..." Perhaps at this moment, the woman straightened and wondered about the identity of this man who knew the words of the God of Israel. She listened intently as Elijah continued, "The jar of flour shall not go empty, nor the jug of oil run dry, until the day when the Lord sends rain upon the earth." With that, the woman did as Elijah instructed. The next day, she opened the jar of flour and noticed that it was full, just as Elijah had said. The same was true of the jar of oil. She was grateful beyond words as she raised her eyes to heaven.

Sometime later, the widow's son fell sick and stopped breathing. In her distress, she blamed Elijah. Once again, he provided comfort and said to her, "Give me your son." He carried the boy's lifeless body to the place where he was staying and placed the boy on his bed. Not knowing what God would do in the situation, Elijah called out in prayer. The Lord heard the prayer of Elijah, and the child was brought back to life. Elijah then carried the child to his mother. Upon seeing her son alive and well, she proclaimed her belief that Elijah was truly "a man of God."[109]

In the meantime, back at the palace, King Ahab recruited Obadiah, a royal master, for a mission to find water in the region. To avoid slaughtering horses and mules, King Ahab was desperate to find grassy areas and water for his animals. Jezebel, on the other hand, was convinced that the prophets of the Lord were responsible for the drought and orchestrated the slaughter of the prophets. To protect the prophets, Obadiah secretly transported one hundred of the prophets to caves in a safe area. He also provided food and water for their survival. During his newly assigned mission to search for water, Obadiah encountered Elijah. King Ahab had searched many nations and kingdoms searching for Elijah. Obadiah could not believe Elijah was standing before him. He reverently bowed before Elijah and asked for confirmation that the man before him was the prophet of the Lord. Elijah confirmed his identity and immediately instructed Obadiah to notify the king of his presence. Fear immediately flooded Obadiah's mind and heart. He was convinced that King Ahab would kill him upon hearing of Elijah's presence. Obadiah even went so far as to remind Elijah of what he had done to ensure the safety of the one hundred prophets. Elijah, however, was determined to present himself to the king. Therefore, Obadiah went to King Ahab and told him of the encounter with Elijah. King Ahab immediately confronted Elijah and, with a brazen tone, said to him, "Is it you, you disturber of Israel?" Without hesitation, Elijah responded boldly, "It is not I who disturb Israel, but you and your father's house, by forsaking the commands of the Lord and you by following the Baals." At that moment, Ahab recognized his guilt and was unable to respond. Elijah then instructed Ahab to summon all of Israel to Mount Carmel, along with all the prophets of Baal and Asherah.[110]

Elijah was focused now more than ever on the God of Israel and the idolatry of His people. Once the people were assembled, Elijah addressed the people boldly and firmly, "How long will you straddle the issue? If the Lord is God, follow him; if Baal, follow him." The people quietly listened to Elijah. Elijah then proclaimed that he was the only remaining prophet of the Lord. He then proposed a challenge to the four hundred and fifty prophets of Baal. "Give us two young bulls. Let them choose one, cut it into pieces, and place it on the wood, but start no fire. I shall prepare the other and place it on the wood but shall start no fire." The people listened intently to these instructions as Elijah continued speaking to the prophets of Baal. "You shall call upon the name of your gods, and I will call upon the name of the Lord. The God who answers with fire is God." The people assembled responded positively to this challenge and agreed that this would be a fair exercise.[111]

After the bulls were prepared as Elijah had instructed, the prophets of Baal began to call upon their gods.

Their cries were unheard, and the sacrifice remained untouched. In their frustration, the prophets of Baal escalated their approach. They prayed louder, demanding that their gods respond to their request. To further indicate the seriousness of their request, they slashed themselves with swords and spears as was customary in their rituals. Despite the intense performance, there was no activity from their gods. "There was no sound, no one answering, no one listening."[112] The people looked at each other with confusion and embarrassment as they turned toward Elijah.

Realizing that all eyes were on him, Elijah began repairing the altar of the Lord. He used twelve stones, which represented the twelve tribes of Israel. He then built a trench around the altar large enough for two measures of grain. He arranged the wood on the altar, cut up the young bull, and placed it on the wood for sacrifice. He then instructed his servants to fill jars with water and pour it over the sacrifice and the wood. The people in the crowd wondered why this was occurring. They spoke among themselves with looks of confusion as they witnessed the preparation of this sacrifice being drenched with water not once but three times as instructed by Elijah.[113]

Once all was in place, Elijah then lifted his eyes toward heaven and prayed:

> *Lord, God of Abraham, Isaac, and Israel, let it be known this day that you are God in Israel and that I am your servant and have done all these things at your command. Answer me, Lord! Answer me, that this people may know that you, Lord, are God and that you have turned their hearts back to you.*
> **1 Kings 18:36**

Immediately following Elijah's prayer, "the Lord's fire came down and devoured the burnt offering, wood, stones, and dust, and lapped up the water in the trench." The people gasped, with their eyes opened wide, as the Lord made Himself known to them. In unison, they prostrated themselves before the altar of the Lord and proclaimed in one voice, "The Lord is God!"[114]

Once again, the one true God of all creation was introduced to the people of Israel. They realized their fallen ways and the disrespect they had shown Him by allowing the gods of Baal and Asherah to enter their land. At that moment, with great boldness, Elijah instructed the people to seize the false prophets and bring them to a specific place in the region known as the Wadi Kishon. At this place, Elijah slaughtered all the prophets of Baal and Asherah. After the death of the false prophets, Elijah instructed King Ahab to "go up, eat and drink, for there is the sound of heavy rain." It had been three years since the last rainfall. Because Ahab knew the importance of the rain, he did as he was told. After Ahab left, Elijah and his servants went to the top of Mount Carmel. Elijah sat on the ground with his head between his knees and recalled all that occurred and the role that he played in God's plan. As he waited for the rain to arrive, Elijah instructed one of his servants to look out to the sea for the approaching rain. Six times, the servant reported no activity. However, on the seventh time, the servant reported seeing "a cloud as small as a man's hand rising from the sea." Elijah knew that this was a sign that the rain was coming. He immediately sent one of his servants to King Ahab's tent, advising him to return home quickly before the rains made it difficult to travel. Before long, "the sky grew dark with clouds and wind, and a heavy rain fell."[115]

King Ahab finally arrived at the palace. He was drenched from the rain. With great joy in his heart, he embraced his wife, Jezebel, and told her of the events of the day. He was thrilled to see rain and knew how this would make life easier for all those in his kingdom. Although the battering of the rain on the roof of the palace brought joy to everyone within its walls, Jezebel was furious that the prophets of her beloved religion had been killed. She wasted no time in getting a message to Elijah. "May the gods do thus to me and more," she wrote, "if by this time tomorrow, I have not done with your life what was done to each of them."[116]

This story, thus far, leads to the Fifth Station of the Eucharist. As we move to the reflection of this station, I choose to proceed in the shoes of Elijah. Elijah was a great prophet. In the New Testament, it is Elijah and Moses who were present during the Transfiguration of Jesus.[117]

In the Transfiguration, Elijah represented the Old Testament prophets, and Moses represented the Old Testament Law. An article in *Catholic Answers Magazine* stated that "these two men...stand in symbolically for the Law and the Prophets: the Old Covenant giving its stamp of approval to the New."[118] Another article stated that not only did Moses and Elijah represent the Law and the Prophets, but "God's voice from heaven – 'Listen to Him!' – clearly showed that the Law and the Prophets must give way to Jesus." The article continued, "The One who is the new and living way is replacing the old – He is the fulfillment of the Law and the countless prophecies in the Old Testament."[119]

The most widely known story of Elijah's life was his miraculous exit to heaven by way of a fiery chariot and horses.[120] Elijah left the earth in a whirlwind and was seen no more until his appearance at the Transfiguration.

There is much to learn from Elijah's life story as we continue with the reflection of this beautiful Station of the Eucharist – *Elijah and the Hearth Cakes.*

Reflection

It is obvious that I have stirred up a huge hornet's nest by doing as God has instructed me. I am only one person, yet God placed me alone against four hundred and fifty false prophets. I am the instrument that God is using to successfully turn the hearts and minds of Ahab and the people of Israel back to God. However, Jezebel is a much bigger challenge. She is now furious, and her husband has no influence over her ability to lash out. I am afraid of what this woman is capable of. I must escape her reach. Together with my servants, we travel to Beer-sheba in the region of Judah. It is not just the distance that is important in reaching Beer-sheba. This city is part of the region of Judah, where Jezebel has no legal authority and, therefore, cannot inflict harm.

After reaching Beer-sheba, I leave my servants and go further into the region of Judah. I am desperate for safety so that I can finally rest. As I walk alone, I think about all that has occurred. *What more could God possibly ask of me?* As I consider the great things God has done so far, not once do I consider His ability to change the heart of Jezebel. The desert is hot and dry, and I have walked several miles on my own. There is no one in sight. I am alone on this road in search of a quiet place to rest. Suddenly, I come upon a broom tree and go directly to the shaded area of the tree. I close my eyes and take a deep breath. As I exhale, I can feel tears well up in my eyes. I fall to my knees and cry out to God, "Enough, Lord! Take my life, for I am no better than my ancestors."[121]

I am exhausted beyond words. Fear has taken hold of me, and I recognize its clench on my thoughts. I feel paralyzed and unable to move any further. Jezebel's death threat is constantly at the forefront of my mind. What is the will of God, and how do I surrender to it if it means that I lose my life by her hand? With tears in my eyes, I lie down and place my satchel under my head. Before long, I fall into a deep sleep.

Suddenly, I sense someone touch my shoulder. I immediately open my eyes. Before me is a young man that I do not recognize. He says, "Get up and eat." As I sit up and turn toward him, I see a hearth cake and a jug of water. I took some provisions from my servants before setting out on my own, but what I have in my satchel is no match for the freshly cooked hearth cake. I try to thank the young man, but he is on his way. I shout to him, "thank you," but he does not seem to hear me. I enjoy the hearth cake and the cold, fresh water. I am still quite tired, so I lay back down and drift off to sleep.[122]

Again, the same young man touches my shoulder. This time, he says quite sternly, "Get up and eat, or the journey will be too much for you!"[123] I realize at that moment that perhaps God sent this man to me. I follow his instructions and eat the food and water made available. I then embark on a long journey to the mountain of God known as Horeb.[124] My heart has always been for the Lord and now more than ever, I want to be close to Him. It was on Mount Horeb, also known as Mount Sinai, where Moses had a special encounter with God. I want and need to be close to Him and so I begin the journey to the mountain of God. It takes forty days and forty nights to reach the mountain. Despite the long journey, I do not experience hunger or thirst. The food provided by the young man under the broom tree seems to suffice. I also realize that the young man is nowhere in sight. It would have been comforting if he had stayed with me. However, this does not seem to be part of God's plan.

Once on the mountaintop, I take refuge in a small cave. I sit quietly in the cave when suddenly, I hear the voice of God ask me a question, "*Why are you here, Elijah?*" Tears immediately well up in my eyes as I hold back the deep cries of grief. I am tired, not so much from the journey to the mountain but from the constant battle with the people of God. I am outnumbered and overwhelmed by the interaction with the Israelites. At times, I feel insignificant and ineffective in everything that I do. I gather my thoughts and respond to God in the best way I know: *"I have been most zealous for the Lord, the God of hosts, but the Israelites have forsaken your covenant. They have destroyed your altars and murdered your prophets by the sword. I alone remain, and they seek to take my life."*[125]

I lower my head in shame, waiting to hear God's response. With love, He simply provides instructions, *"Go out and stand on the mountain before the Lord; the Lord will pass by."*[126] Although my goal is to get close to God, I begin to feel nervous about the encounter. *What would happen to me in the presence of God Almighty? Will I survive this encounter? What will I see? How should I react?* I stand nervously on this mountain, waiting for the Lord. Suddenly, in sequence, three dramatic manifestations occur. First, there is a strong, violent wind that is crushing rocks all around me. I do my best to stand in place and shield my eyes from the sand that is tossed around by the wind. *Is this God?* I wonder. This force is certainly powerful.

Despite the energy surrounding me, my heart knows that God is not in the wind.

The wind dies down, and there is a short moment of peace when suddenly the earth begins to move. I fall to my knees and brace myself as crevices begin to form all around me. This is a mighty force and yet again, I know in my heart that God is not in this event.

Because I know of the power and greatness of God, it is always my expectation that God would present Himself in a mighty force like wind or an earthquake. However, that is not the case. Despite the intensity of these forces, God is not in them. As I wonder how He will present Himself, a great fire begins to stir up all around me. I immediately recall the challenge between the God of Israel and the gods of Baal. The fire that consumed the sacrifice on the altar after I prayed for God's intervention is like this fire that consumes all that is in its path. Perhaps God will manifest Himself in the fire. However, the flames of this fire are higher than I have ever experienced, and the intensity of the heat is almost too much to bear. I shield my face as I look intently into the fire all around me. However, God is not in the fire. I know this in the depths of my heart. The fire ceases, and there is a silence that makes me wonder what will happen next.[127]

As I straighten, I can hear a light, silent sound. It is the sweetest and calmest sound I have ever heard. I position my head toward the sound so I can hear it better. It is so peaceful. Suddenly I can sense the presence of God. I hide my face in my cloak and move to the entrance of the cave. The peacefulness is still there when I hear the gentle whisper of God ask again, *"Why are you here, Elijah?"* I respond in the same way as I did earlier. However, this time, God provides specific instructions. I am to go back by a designated route to the city of Damascus. While there, I am to anoint a new king of Aram. I am also instructed to anoint a new king for Israel. God's instructions also provide the name of my replacement, Elisha, son of Shaphat of Abel-meholah. God's plan unfolds in the still, small voice and in a gentle whisper. His plan includes the protection of seven thousand in Israel who have not worshipped the false gods of Baal.[128] Although I know I will be replaced by Elisha, I am looking forward to seeing God's plan unfold in my life. The still, small voice has had a tremendous impact on my heart. I know I will share this experience with Elisha as I train him to continue the work that God has planned for him.

++++++++++

It is now time to consider the exhaustion and depression experienced by Elijah as he sat under the broom tree. Have you ever experienced this type of despair in your life? If so, what caused these feelings? And what did you do to overcome them?

As you consider Elijah's experiences, do you think he would have reached the mountain of God and encountered God in the still, small voice if he refused the food provided by the young man under the broom tree? Do you see the correlation between the hearth cake provided under the broom tree and the Eucharist provided at every Mass? The Eucharist is Jesus and the "source and summit of the Christian life," as noted in the *Catechism of the Catholic Church.*[129] The Eucharist is the special meal that God provides for us as we rest under the broom tree, which signifies His Church. Prayerfully consider the intimacy of this special meal and the assistance Jesus provides as you journey through life.

PRAYER NOTES

PRAYER NOTES

Chapter 6

Bethlehem - The House of Bread

Chapter 6

Bethlehem – The House of Bread

Bethlehem is an interesting city. It is the birthplace of Our Lord and Savior, Jesus Christ. However, it was not until this writing that I had the opportunity to dig into the history of Bethlehem.

The name *Bethlehem* in Aramaic means *House of Bread*.[130] However, in the Jewish dictionary, the name Bethlehem means both *House of Bread* and *House of War*. "The first part of the name Bethlehem," according to the *Jewish Dictionary*, "means *house*...The second part comes from the curious root group *laham*, meaning either *make war* or *use as food*. The verb *laham* means to fight or do battle and is used frequently in the Bible...This verb also means to eat or use as food."[131] In Arabic, according to an article by Father Patrick Briscoe, the name Bethlehem means *House of Meat*.[132]

Bethlehem is located five miles south of Jerusalem. Standing at an elevation of about 2,500 feet above the sea, Bethlehem is 100 feet higher than Jerusalem. Its climate is mild, and rainfall is plentiful, resulting in fertile fields, orchards, and vineyards.[133] Bethlehem is in the hill country of Judah and was originally called *Ephrath*, which means *fruitful*. It is also referred to as *Bethlehem-Ephratah, Bethlehem-Judah*, and the *City of David*.[134] David was born in Bethlehem and was also anointed in this city as king of Israel by Samuel, as noted in the Book of Samuel in the Old Testament.[135]

The first mention of Ephrath, the original name for Bethlehem, occurs in the Book of Genesis in reference to the place where Rachel died giving birth to Benjamin and was buried on the road from Bethel.[136] Boaz was also from Bethlehem and is mentioned in the Book of Ruth.[137] Boaz married Ruth, a Gentile woman, and welcomed her into his Jewish family. Both Boaz and Ruth are mentioned in the genealogy of Jesus in the Gospel of Matthew.[138] David, Israel's greatest king, shepherded sheep in the fields of Bethlehem. Most importantly, however, the city of Bethlehem is connected to the messianic prophecy, as noted in the Book of Micah. Several passages from a variety of ancient Jewish writings have made it clear that at least some Jews considered the fifth chapter of the Book of Micah to be a Messianic prophecy.[139]

> *But you, Bethlehem-Ephrathah least among the clans of Judah, from you shall come forth for me one who is to be ruler in Israel; whose origin is from old, from ancient times. Therefore the Lord will give them up, until the time when she who is to give birth has borne, then the rest of his kindred shall return to the children of Israel.* **Micah 5:1-2**

The birth of Jesus is noted in both the Gospels of Matthew and Luke. The common elements of the birth of Jesus presented in these gospels, according to Father Felix Just, S.J., Ph.D., include the main characters, *Mary, Joseph, and Jesus*, as well as supporting characters: *angels and the Holy Spirit*. Jesus was noted in these gospels as *Christ, son of David*. His ancestry included the *children of Abraham and the house of David*. The historical period for the birth of Jesus, as noted in both Gospels, is *during the reign of King Herod*.[140]

Father Just also pointed out the different contents of the biblical accounts of the birth of Jesus. For example, the Gospel of Matthew began with the genealogy of Jesus. However, the Gospel of Luke mentions the genealogy in its third chapter. The Gospel of Luke detailed the Annunciation by the Angel Gabriel to the Blessed Mother as well as the Visitation to Elizabeth, the birth and circumcision of John the Baptist, and the journey to Bethlehem by Joseph and Mary for the census. At the beginning of the Gospel of Matthew, the only reference to an angel was the announcement made to Joseph in a dream regarding the birth of Jesus. Both gospels stated clearly that Mary gave birth to a son in Bethlehem of Judea and that her son's name was Jesus. In the Gospel of Luke, shepherds visited the infant Jesus lying in a manger. This Gospel also told of the presentation of Our Lord in the temple and included the proclamation from both Simeon and Anna. Although this event was not included in the Gospel of Matthew, he did include the visit from the Magi and the interaction with King Herod. Both Gospels indicated that the Holy Family left Bethlehem and returned to Nazareth.[141]

It was within the story of the Magi in the Gospel of Matthew that reference is made to the words provided by the prophet, Micah. The Magi arrived in Jerusalem in search of the king of the Jews. They approached King Herod, asking for the whereabouts of this newborn king. King Herod gathered the chief priests and scribes and asked them where the Messiah was to be born. It was at this time that they quoted the prophet Micah. He is to be born "in Bethlehem of Judea," they acclaimed. "For thus it has been written through the prophet: And you, Bethlehem, land of Judah, are by no means least among the rulers of Judah; since from you shall come a ruler, who is to shepherd my people, Israel."[142]

In response to a question regarding the place of Jesus' birth, Saint Thomas Aquinas responded in the *Summa Theologica* that "Christ willed to be born in Bethlehem for two reasons. First, because 'He was made...of the seed of David according to the flesh.'" According to Saint Thomas, "He willed to be born at Bethlehem, where David was born, in order that by the very birthplace the promise made to David might be shown to be fulfilled." In addition, Saint Thomas reminded the reader that "Bethlehem is interpreted as *the house of bread*.'" He then connected its meaning to the words of Christ in the Gospel of John, "I am the living Bread that came down from heaven."[143]

Bethlehem is also known as the birthplace of the Eucharist. Pope Saint John Paul II, in a homily for Midnight Mass in 2004, stated, "In Bethlehem was born the One who, under the sign of broken bread, would leave us the memorial of his Pasch. On this Holy Night, adoration of the Child Jesus becomes Eucharistic adoration. We adore you, Lord, truly present in the Sacrament of the Altar, the living Bread which gives life to humanity. We acknowledge you as our one God, a little Child lying helpless in the manger!" Pope Saint John Paul II continued with a quote from Saint Irenaeus, "In the fullness of time, you became a man among men, to unite the end to the beginning, that is, man to God." In the conclusion of his homily, Pope Saint John Paul II stated, "You are born on this Night, our divine Redeemer, and, in our journey along the paths of time, you become for us the food of eternal life."[144]

"In the Eucharist," as noted in an article by Father Patrick Briscoe, "Jesus Christ is present to us in time, just as he was present to holy Mary and Saint Joseph at the moment he was born." "Every place the Mass is offered," according to Father Briscoe, "is transformed into a sort of Bethlehem, a place where heaven touches earth, where Christ becomes our food." One of the most controversial Scriptures in the New Testament is found in the Gospel of John, Chapter 6. Jesus clearly stated in verse 55 of this chapter that "my flesh is true food, and my blood is true drink. Whoever eats my flesh and drinks my blood remains in me, and I in him."[145] Shortly after his birth, Jesus was wrapped in swaddling clothes and placed in a manger.[146] A manger, according to the *Merriam-Webster Dictionary*, "is a trough or open box in a stable designed to hold feed or fodder for livestock."[147] Saint Ambrose of Milan connected the manger in Luke's Gospel to the Scripture in the Old Testament by the prophet Isaiah. *"An ox knows its owner, and an ass, its master's manger; But Israel does not know, my people has not understood."*[148] In the article by Father Briscoe, he concluded that "as it was the case of old, there are many today who do not recognize Christ, the Eucharistic food, who was placed in the manger!"[149]

In 330 A.D., Constantine the Great built the *Church of the Nativity* over the grotto or cave called the *holy crypt,* which was said to be the *stable* in which Jesus was born.[150] The original church was destroyed in a fire during the Samaritan revolts of the sixth century. A new basilica was built years later by Byzantine Emperor, Justinian.[151] There was a 14-point Silver Star placed beneath the altar that indicated the specific place of Jesus' birth.[152] This grotto is the oldest site continuously used as a place of worship in Christianity. Since 2012, the Church of the Nativity has been a World Heritage Site and was the first to be listed by the United Nations Education, Scientific, and Cultural Organization (UNESCO) under Palestine.[153]

Reflection

As I consider the town of Bethlehem in this Sixth Station of the Eucharist, I am reminded of a December visit to Saint Leo Abbey, a Benedictine monastery, an hour's drive from my home in Florida. Saint Leo Abbey traces its roots back to 1882. The Abbey church was commissioned to be built in 1935 and was consecrated in January 1948.[154] The church, at the time of my visit, was beautifully decorated for Christmas. As I approached the main altar, I noticed a section to the left that displayed a beautiful nativity scene. The creche was always part of my childhood Christmas. In my home, it was the last item to be placed under the tree. The Christmas decorations were not complete until the creche was in its place.

As a child, my family visited Saint Patrick's Cathedral in New York City every year. We would begin our adventure with a stroll down Fifth Avenue, admiring all the beautifully decorated window displays. We would then enter Saint Patrick's Cathedral and wait in line to see the nativity scene. I remember one year realizing that the baby Jesus in this creche was the same size as my little brother, who was born several months earlier. Throughout the years, I have seen many different-sized creches, but always the same people were displayed. The Blessed Mother, Saint Joseph, and baby Jesus were always at the center of the creche. An angel was displayed above them. Around the manger where the baby Jesus lay, there were shepherds, three wise men, sheep, and sometimes a camel or two. However, my experience at Saint Leo Abbey was quite different.

The nativity scene displayed at Saint Leo Abbey depicted the entire town of Bethlehem. I had never seen anything this detailed before. There were three tables positioned in a horseshoe. I knew I wanted to see everything, so I began with the table to my right. The display began with chariots and guards and a tower indicating the protection provided for its residents. As I continued looking carefully at each section, I noticed the daily activities of the people of

Bethlehem. There were women washing clothes and cooking meals, men tending sheep, and children playing in the fields. There was a market displaying beautiful fruits, vegetables, blankets, and other home goods, with men and women buying and selling items needed for their lives in Bethlehem. The housing was also on display. Some were large with detailed designs. Others were small shanties that barely provided cover from the elements. Animals were also part of this detailed display. There were dogs that helped with the sheep, as well as donkeys and elephants that assisted with carrying goods from place to place. The greenery, rocks, and hills in the display also helped portray the reality of life in Bethlehem at the time of Jesus' birth.

As I moved slowly toward the center of the main table, I recognized the familiar nativity scene from my youth. There, amid everyday life in Bethlehem, Our Lord and Savior was born. He was then wrapped in swaddling clothes and laid in a manger. The news of his birth must have traveled extensively throughout the town.

I consider the challenge of Saint Ignatius of Loyola to place myself in the scene. In this challenge, Saint Ignatius asks us to consider what it would be like to be one of the main characters or a bystander. There are so many options as I consider the many activities in the town of Bethlehem. Our imagination can take us through different possible scenes within the context of the station or scripture presented. As I consider the challenge, I choose to place myself in the scene as a bystander, more specifically, as the wife of one of the shepherds of Bethlehem.

During my everyday duties, I learn from one of my neighbors that a very pregnant woman and her husband have been turned down at the local inn. "Where did they go?" I ask. One of the women says she heard that they had to bed down in one of the caves. "Did she have her baby there?" I then ask. "I think so," one of the women says. She then remarks that "there were shepherds that talked about a special newborn that they visited during their night watch." That evening, I ask my husband if he knows anything about this abandoned family. He says he heard the story from other shepherds but did not witness any of it himself. Bethlehem is a bustling town. There are so many people coming and going. We hear stories all the time about people who need shelter. The inn is constantly full of travelers, and often, people are turned away. But this is the first time I have heard of a pregnant woman experiencing rejection for shelter. I look closely at my two-year-old son. It wasn't long ago that I gave birth. My delivery was long and challenging since it was my first child. However, I was surrounded by an experienced midwife, my mother, and two other women who helped with the birth. I wonder what this woman experienced in the darkness of a cave. I also think of her child and wonder what she might need to properly care for him.

As I get my family ready for the start of a new day, I notice a small baby blanket given to me by a neighbor when my child was first born. Although my child has outgrown the size of the blanket, it can still be used by another. I tuck the blanket in my belt and head toward the market located near the cave where the woman and her husband were said to be. I purchase a few items in the market for my family and then head toward the cave.

At the entrance, I see a cow and donkey grazing on the grass. As I get closer, I notice a woman busy with daily chores. I clear my voice so that she knows I am there. She immediately turns and looks towards me. I am stunned by her beauty. She is also very young. I notice from her clothing that she is no longer pregnant. I introduce myself, and she smiles sweetly. "Were you the woman turned down by the inn for shelter?" I ask. She smiles and nods in affirmation. "Did you have your baby?" I ask. She then turns toward one of the mangers in the cave. My heart skips a beat as I think of a baby being placed in a manger. I walk slowly toward the manger and look in. What a beautiful sight. The child is just as beautiful as his mother. The manger is also beautifully lined with hay and a blanket.

I sit with this mother for a little while. Over tea, we talk about our experiences. There is something special about this young woman. We are nearing the end of our conversation when her husband arrives with supplies from the market. He, too, smiles at me as we make eye contact. I then stand up and say my final goodbyes. As I walk away, I remember the blanket. "Oh, I almost forgot," I say with surprise. "This was given to me when my son was born," I explain. "He is too big for it now. Maybe you can use it for your son." The woman accepts the gift with great joy. Before leaving, I walk to the manger and say my goodbyes to the beautiful child.

As I make my way home, I wonder what, if any, is the significance of this family who sought shelter in a cave. How brave this woman was to travel the way she did. I was born and raised in Bethlehem and never ventured outside its walls. We did not talk about why she traveled in her condition or where she intended to go from here. Suddenly, I remember what my friend told me about the shepherds who visited the newborn during their night watch. I was close to one of the fields where sheep were grazing. I see a shepherd and decide to ask him if he knows about what had occurred the night the child was born. To my surprise, the shepherd was one of the visitors. In detail, he explains the host of angels that appeared the night the child was born. He also shares how he and the others were struck with great fear. It was an angel who calmed their fears and proclaimed to them "good news of great joy that will be for all the people."[155] It was then explained to the shepherds that a Savior had been born, who is the Messiah and Lord. My eyes widen in unbelief. The shepherd continues, "The angel told us that we would find an infant wrapped in swaddling clothes and lying in a manger."[156] I then exclaim, "I just visited the woman in the cave, and what you describe is what I saw – a beautiful baby wrapped in swaddling clothes and lying in a manger." "Yes," the shepherd says. "That is what we saw when we arrived at the cave that night." The shepherd continues, "The amazing thing about this was that after the angels told us what we would see, we heard them all singing and praising God saying: 'Glory to God in the highest and on Earth peace to those on whom his favor rests.'"[157]

I close my eyes in wonder and then continue my walk home. I then remember the beauty of the infant. Could this be the Messiah? Could I have been that close and not known who was near?

++++++++++

Our lives are very busy with the demands of everyday living. Do we see the significance of the Lord being placed in the manger? Do we recognize that the celebration of Christmas is not only the celebration of Jesus' birth but also the celebration of the birthplace of the Eucharist?

Jesus provides food for our journey of life. Do we recognize Him? Do we make room for Him, or are we too busy living life to acknowledge all that He has done and is currently doing in our lives?

As you contemplate further this Sixth Station of the Eucharist, prayerfully consider the manger, the Eucharist, and all that it represents.

PRAYER NOTES

PRAYER NOTES

Chapter 7

The Wedding Feast at Cana

Chapter 7

The Wedding Feast at Cana

As I began my research for this Seventh Station of the Eucharist, I discovered an article posted on a Christian website that stated that "Jesus often used Jewish marriage customs as a beautiful allegory of God's relationship with the church, His 'bride.'"[158] This sparked my curiosity regarding the celebration that took place during Jesus' first miracle. *What were wedding celebrations like in biblical times, and what, if anything, was the significance of the wine at these celebrations?*

The Jewish wedding ceremonies of today include a canopy under which the bride and groom declare their love and commitment to one another. However, this tradition came "hundreds of years after Jesus died on the cross..."[159] According to an article by Steve Rudd, "There were three stages of a marriage in the Bible." The first stage was the signing of the *ketubah* contract. This contract created the marriage bond. Once signed, the couple were legally married even though the relationship had not yet been consummated.[160]

An article by Monsignor Charles Pope indicated that "marriage took place at a very young age for the ancient Jews." The proposed age for men, according to Pope's article, was age 18, "though often a bit younger, especially when war was less common." "Young women," he continued, "married almost as soon as they were physically ready for marriage, approximately age 13 or 14." Monsignor Pope further stated that "in most cases, marriages were arranged by the parents for their children" and that "marriage was not so much about love and romance as it was about survival."[161]

The second stage of marriage, according to ancient Jewish wedding customs, was called the *chuppah*. This was the sexual consummation of marriage. The groom, according to Rudd's article, had up to seven years to raise the money, as noted in the *ketubah* contract. The contract details were negotiated between the families prior to the signing of the *ketubah*.[162] The amount to be paid by the groom and his family was known as the *mohar*. In addition, the groom provided a gift to the bride known as the *mattan*. The gift was not always monetary and sometimes included property or services provided to the bride's family.[163] Once all the details of the contract were attained, the groom would notify the father of the bride. A date would then be set "to consummate the marriage at the bride's home." The bride, not knowing the day and time of the groom's arrival, waited patiently with her maidservants.[164]

Today, the *chuppah* is a canopy under which a Jewish couple stands during their wedding ceremony. The canopy consists of a cloth or sheet stretched or supported over four poles. A *chuppah* symbolizes the home that the couple will build together. However, in biblical times, the *chuppah* was the name given to a room or tent where the marriage was consummated.[165] While in the *chuppah* room, the families of the couple and their friends would celebrate outside or in the next room. In preparing the *chuppah* room, the mother of the bride or the bride herself would sew the name of the couple and possibly the date of the consummation onto a cloth about two feet square. This was called the *proof of virginity cloth* that the bride would lie upon during the consummation. Also, prior to this event, formal witnesses were assigned by both families. These witnesses waited outside the chuppah room. It was the groom's responsibility after the consummation to hand the special blood-stained cloth to the witnesses, who would then present it to the father of the bride as proof of her virginity. After the consummation, the bride and groom, along with their families and others in the wedding party, processed to the house of the groom for a *wedding feast*. This was the third stage of marriage noted in Rudd's article.[166]

In the Old Testament, these three stages were evident in the marriage of Isaac to Rebekah. In the Book of Genesis, Abraham sent his servant to "get a wife for my son, Isaac."[167] The servant met Rebekah and then made an offer of marriage to her father, Bethuel. The offer was accepted, and Rebekah was married by the acceptance of her father to the proposed union. Gifts were then presented to Rebekah, her parents, and her brother. Rebekah then left with Abraham's servant to meet her new husband. As they approached the region where Isaac lived, Rebekah "caught sight of Isaac and got down from her camel." She asked the servant as to the identity of the man before them. "That is my master," replied the servant. Then, Rebekah "took her veil and covered herself." The servant then recounted to Isaac all that had been done as instructed by his father, Abraham. Isaac then "brought Rebekah into the tent of his mother, Sarah. He took Rebekah as his wife."[168] Although there was no mention of a wedding feast, Rudd noted in his article that "one likely happened."

The three stages of marriage, however, can be easily noted in the marriage of Jacob to both Leah and Rachel. This story was detailed in the Old Testament in the Book of Genesis. Although Jacob's original intent was to marry Rachel, he was tricked by his father-in-law to marry Leah. Upon realizing the deception, Jacob confronted his father-in-law, who explained that "it is not the custom in our country to give the younger daughter before the firstborn." The father-in-law then instructed Jacob to "finish the bridal week" for Leah, and then "the other [Rachel] will also be given to you in return for another seven years of service with me."[169] The *bridal week* referred to the *wedding feast,* and the *seven years of service* was the *marriage contract.*

Jesus' first miracle took place at a wedding feast in Cana. Nathaniel, also known as Bartholemew, was one of Jesus' apostles. Nathaniel was from Cana and perhaps knew the bride and groom at this wedding feast. The *ketubah* contract for this couple had already been agreed upon. The groom had also fulfilled the requirements in the contract and the marriage had been consummated. The week-long wedding celebration was underway when Mary, Jesus' mother, noticed that there was no more wine.[170]

In the Book of Genesis, Isaac provided a blessing to his son, Jacob. In the blessing, he stated, "May God give to you of the dew of the heavens and of the fertility of the earth abundance of grain and wine."[171] In an article by Mary Fairchild, she noted that wine in the Old Testament "symbolized life and vitality. It was a sign of joy, blessing, and prosperity." Fairfield also stated that "throughout the Old Testament, partaking of wine was associated with happiness and celebration." "In addition," she noted, "the Israelites were commanded to make drink offerings of wine and tithes of wine."[172] An article by Zachary Garris reminded us of the first station of the Eucharist when Melchizedek blessed Abraham with the gifts of bread and wine. Garris further stated that "wine is a sign of God's blessing because it is associated with feasting, as well as Sabbath rest and relaxation."[173]

The absence of wine at a wedding celebration in Jesus' time would be an embarrassment to the groom's family. Mary knew this and immediately shared her concern with Jesus. As I thought about the conversation between Mary and Jesus at this wedding celebration, I considered that they might be talking on different planes. By this, I mean that Mary was sharing her observations of the wedding that was occurring at that moment. However, Jesus was responding on a different level. When Mary stated the obvious that "there is no more wine," Jesus responded by calling her *Woman* rather than *Mother*. In doing this, he acknowledged Mary as the New Eve. He also acknowledged that His hour had not yet come. He is the bridegroom of the Church, and He knows His responsibility to provide the wine for the wedding feast. Mary might not have fully understood His words, but she knew Her Son could help. So, she turned to the servers and said, "Do whatever He tells you." Do you think Jesus rolled his eyes when He heard his mother speak to the servers? I certainly considered this. There were many times I rolled my eyes at what I considered odd requests from my mother. However, this was not an odd request. Jesus understood the importance of wine not only for the wedding feast but for the blessings it brought to the people in the Old Testament. He also knew the important role wine would play in His passion. He, therefore, responded to His mother's request by providing detailed instructions to the servers.

Now, there were six stone water jars there for Jewish ceremonial washings, each holding twenty to thirty gallons. Jesus told them, "Fill the jars with water." So they filled them to the brim. Then he told them, "Draw some out now and take it to the headwaiter." So they took it. And when the headwaiter tasted the water that had become wine, without knowing where it came from (although the servers who had drawn the water knew), the headwaiter called the bridegroom and said to him, "Everyone serves good wine first, and then when people have drunk freely, an inferior one; but you have kept the good wine until now." Jesus did this as the beginning of his signs in Cana in Galilee and so revealed his glory, and his disciples began to believe in him. **John 2:6-11**

Reflection

As I contemplate this Station of the Eucharist and the information attained regarding the different stages of marriage in the Bible, I place myself in this scene as one of the female witnesses assigned by the bride's family. I have known the bride since childhood. We played together as children and learned the many duties of caring for a family. It is an honor to be selected as a witness for this special occasion. My friend and I have talked many times about becoming mothers. Marriage, we learned, would be the first step toward reaching that goal.

I meet the other women who are chosen by the bride's family to witness the event. I know most of them and soon become re-acquainted. I am also introduced to new women in the bridal party. It is quite exciting. The time of day of the groom's arrival is not known. To prepare, we each are given lamps with a small supply of oil. To ensure we would have enough oil for the event, we each acquire more from our families before assembling outside the chuppah room.

It is very late in the evening when the groom arrives with his friends. I am grateful to have the extra oil. I have already refilled my lamp and wait patiently with the others for his arrival. As the groom makes his way to the area where we are standing, the male witnesses announce his arrival with the sound of the *shofar*. The *shofar* is a ram horn that is used as a trumpet for special occasions such as this one. I've heard it many times during Rosh Hashanah, the Jewish New Year, and Yom Kippur, also known as the Day of Atonement. We are all so happy to see the groom. Since I am standing near the door of the *chuppah* room, I gently knock on the door and announce happily to the bride that, "The groom is here!" I can only imagine the happiness of my friend as she waits for her beloved. At the same time, I know she must be feeling apprehension for what is to occur.

As the groom enters the *chuppah* room, we move closer to the fire. We begin singing songs and enjoy the peacefulness of the evening. I do not recall how much time passes by when suddenly the groom calls one of his friends. Immediately, we stop singing and focus our attention on the door of the *chuppah*. Three of the groom's friends go quickly to the door. The door opens slightly, and the groom hands his friend a cloth. Although this is my first time as a witness for this type of event, I have heard so many stories from my mother and aunts. I know the meaning of the cloth and immediately clapped my hands with great joy. I am not alone in doing so. We are all happy for the couple. As the cloth is being presented to the bride's father, my eyes are fixed on the door. I cannot wait to see my friend. Suddenly, the door opens, and both the bride and groom come forward. My friend's face is radiant with joy and happiness. I am so happy for her.

With our lamps in hand, we process with the bride and groom, their families, and all the witnesses to the groom's house, where the entire village is waiting for the celebration to begin.

The party is being held in a large room at the groom's home. There is so much joy and happiness in the room. As I enter, my eyes scan the room. There are beautiful decorations everywhere. I recognize some of them as I watched my mother and aunts, days and weeks prior, help with the preparations. Several musicians are on hand. Upon seeing the bride and groom, the musicians perform an uplifting rendition that has everyone on their feet and clapping joyfully. As is our tradition, the men and women are separated into two different spaces. A curtain separates the large room, designating one side for men and the other for women. This separation lasts only a few hours. It is fun to dance with the bride and all the other women in our families. However, I am anxious to see who is on the other side of the curtain. Before long, the curtain is removed, and the festivities continue with great joy. Almost immediately, I see my friend, Nathaniel. I make my way through the crowd to where he is standing. We embrace each other warmly, and then he introduces me to Jesus, his mother, and his other close friends.

We are having so much fun at this celebration. There is dancing and food at every table. As in many of our celebrations, wine is shared by all, and it is quite good. As I leave the dance floor and head toward the table with my friends, I notice the servers talking among themselves as they look inside the large jars of wine. There is obviously a problem. Mary notices it, too. She then speaks to her son, Jesus, who then provides instructions to the servants. I do not know the particulars of what Jesus has said to the servers; however, one of the servers, as instructed by Jesus, takes a cup, fills it with water from the ceremonial jars, and brings it to the head waiter. I thought this was very odd. By now, Nathaniel is standing next to me. I then ask him, "Do you know what is going on?" As we carefully watch the server approach the headwaiter, Nathaniel replies, "I'm not sure." After a few words with the server, the headwaiter takes a sip of the liquid in the cup. The expression on the headwaiter's face indicates that the liquid is more than water. He is quite pleased and surprised at its content. I immediately turn to Nathaniel and ask, "What is in the ceremonial jars?" The frown on Nathaniel's face is evidence that he is as confused as I am about the situation. The servers are busy filling the pitchers with the liquid from the jars. I get closer and realize that the liquid being poured into the pitchers is not water. I then turn to Nathaniel and say, "We should try some of this." Nathaniel reaches toward one of the tables and returns with two empty cups. He then gets closer to one of the ceremonial jars and pours the liquid from the jar to each cup. We know at this point that it is wine. We look at each other and then take our first sip of the wine. I have never tasted anything so wonderful in my life. From the expression on his face, neither has Nathaniel. We are so taken aback by the richness of this wine and its distinct flavors. I then turn toward Jesus. As I watch Him enjoying Himself with his friends, I wonder about who He is and why He performed this special miracle for my friend and her new husband.

++++++++++

As you contemplate this Station of the Eucharist, consider the perspective of the headwaiter. Do you think he investigated the matter further and discovered that it was Jesus who was responsible for the fine wine? What do you think the headwaiter would say to Jesus about this miracle? What would you say to Jesus about this miracle?

Consider further the preparation of the witnesses for the bride and groom. Would you be prepared even if the groom showed up very late in the evening? Would you have prepared in advance to obtain extra oil for your lamp? Prayerfully consider the ways you prepare to receive Jesus in the Eucharist.

PRAYER NOTES

PRAYER NOTES

Chapter 8

The Multiplication of the Loaves

Chapter 8

The Multiplication of the Loaves

The *Multiplication of the Loaves*, as noted in an article by Father Satish Joseph, is the "only miracle found in all four Gospels." In the Gospel of Matthew, Father Joseph noted that the difference between Herod's banquet held immediately prior to the murder of John the Baptist and the banquet provided by Jesus was the multiplication of the loaves. Father Joseph pointed out that "at Herod's banquet, we see false pride, arrogance, victimization of the righteous, the misuse of power, and murder." However, at Jesus' banquet, he noted, "There is compassion, healing, trust, and sharing." Jesus operated from compassion, which, according to Father Joseph, was "the key principle to interpreting the rest of the multiplication story."[174] Compassion, as noted in an article by Opus Dei, "is not simply feeling pity; it's more! It means to suffer with, in other words, to empathize with the suffering of another, to the point of taking it upon oneself."[175]

As the crowd gathered, Jesus recognized their human need for food. He refused, however, to send them away. Jesus used the opportunity, according to Father Joseph, "to train his disciples in the school of compassion." In doing so, Jesus said to His disciples, "Give them some food yourselves."[176] I can envision the dumbfounded look on the disciples' faces as they consider the logistics needed to fulfill Jesus' request. Finally, they stated the obvious, "Five loaves and two fish are all we have here."[177] Jesus then instructed them to bring what they had to Him. Jesus was teaching them the importance of giving. It is our hearts that must be willing to give no matter how little we have. This was where the miracle began.

Once Jesus received the offering of the five loaves and two fish, He then looked "up to heaven, said the blessing, broke the loaves, and gave them to the disciples, who in turn gave them to the crowds."[178] In Father Joseph's article, he stated that the "Multiplication of the loaves and fish is a fulfillment of Isaiah's prophecy."[179]

> *All you who are thirsty, come to the water. You who have no money, come, buy grain and eat; Come, buy grain without money, wine and milk without cost! Why spend your money for what is not bread, your wages for what does not satisfy? Only listen to me, and you shall eat well, you shall delight in rich fare.* **Isaiah 55:1-2**

Father Joseph further stated that this miracle of multiplication was "a vision into our future eternal life with God in heaven." Another important part of this miracle was that there were twelve baskets of leftovers, reminding us of the free abundance of grace available to each of us. "This table of plenty," as noted by Father Joseph, "is the Eucharistic table."[180]

This miracle also showed the importance of human cooperation. God is more than able to provide this miracle without human participation. However, when Jesus asked the disciples to "give them some food yourselves," He provided an opportunity for the transformation of their hearts, resulting in a miracle at a much deeper level. Saint Josemaria Escriva stated that God "does not need any of us, and at the same time, he needs us all." "What a marvelous thing this is!" he continued. "He (Jesus) is asking us for the little we are, the little we are worth, for our few talents. We cannot hold back anything from him. The two fishes, the bread – everything."[181] In 2016, Pope Francis, in response to the miracle of the multiplication of the loaves, stated that "Jesus allows his disciples to carry out his command. In this way, they know the path to follow: to feed the people and keep them united; that is, to be at the service of life and of communion."[182]

In the Gospel of John, upon seeing the large crowds, Jesus singled out Philip and asked him, "Where can we buy enough food for them to eat?" Philip then stated the obvious, "Two hundred days' wages worth of food would not be enough for each of them to have a little bit."[183] In other words, Philip was stating that *we do not have the money or the resources for all of them*. Perhaps Andrew overheard the conversation between Jesus and Philip. To help his friend, Philip, resolve the issue Jesus was presenting, Andrew pointed out that there is "a boy here who has five barley loaves and two fish." Andrew, however, agreed with Philip and added the comment, "But what good are these for so many?"[184]

Jesus then asked Philip, Andrew, and the other disciples to instruct the crowd to *recline.* The word *recline* was used in several Scripture translations. Jesus said, in verse ten of the sixth chapter of the Gospel of John, "Have the people *recline.*"[185] Other Scripture translations use the word *sit.* "Then Jesus said, make the people *sit* down."[186] The word *recline* seems to be the most appropriate translation. An article titled *Table Manners and Christianity* provided a better understanding of the customs of Jesus' time. The article stated that lying down to eat was a custom in the Middle East, Greece, and Rome. This custom lasted for more than one thousand years. Not until the end of the Western Roman Empire were beds abandoned in favor of chairs.[187] It was evident that Jesus not only wanted the crowd in a comfortable, relaxed position, but He also wanted them ready to eat. He was going to feed them and, therefore, wanted them in the customary position to receive a meal. Once the 5,000 men were reclined and ready for the meal, Jesus then "took the loaves, gave thanks, and distributed them to those who were reclining, and also as much of the fish as they wanted."[188]

In an article about the *Multiplication of the Loaves*, Donagh O'Shea addressed the significance of the bread that was given. Scripture indicated that the young boy had five barley loaves. O'Shea stated that barley loaves were "the cheapest kind of bread" and further stated that "barley was considered animal feed." "Only the very poor," he continued, "would eat barley loaves." O'Shea pointed out two main effects of poverty. Poverty, he said, "can turn people in on themselves, filling them with resentment and self-pity; or it can turn them outwards to a real experience of God's Providence." "Poverty," he continued, "can break people's spirit, which is why it is so important to fight against it." In this article, O'Shea also stated that "when we are at the Eucharist, we are those disciples in John 6, sitting on the ground, in humility and simplicity, sharing our poverty and sharing the Lord's gift."[189]

Father Daniel Callam, in an article from *Catholic Insight*, pointed out that "there are two (stories) of the multiplication of the loaves" featured in the Gospels of Matthew and Mark. In the Gospel of Mark, "the first" (story), stated Father Callam, "came after the raising from the dead of the daughter of Jairus."[190] Immediately following the raising of Jairus' daughter, Jesus said that "she should be given something to eat."[191] Jesus gave the same instructions to His disciples when faced with a large crowd. He told them to "give them some food yourselves."[192] This multiplication miracle fed 5,000, and the remaining fragments filled twelve baskets. The second multiplication miracle fed 4,000. This second miracle, as noted by Father Callam, took place "after the cure of the possessed daughter of the Syro-Phoenician woman."[193] The location of these miracles and the numbers associated with each brought about a deeper understanding. For example, in an article by *Lo & Behold*, it was noted that Jesus performed the first multiplication miracle "in Bethsaida, which is Jewish territory." In this first miracle, "There were five loaves divided and twelve baskets of leftovers." The article stated that "the five loaves symbolized the five books of the Torah," and the fragments left over symbolized the "twelve tribes of Israel."[194] Father Callam further explained that the Torah, represented by the number five in this miracle, "establish the covenant that constituted the Jews as the people of God." Father Callam also provided further explanation regarding the twelve baskets remaining. This, he said, signified that "there is enough bread for an entire nation." In conclusion, Father Callam stated that "we are led, therefore, to looking upon the feeding as a symbol of the Messianic banquet, that is to say, of the Messianic era." Therefore, it is noted that "Jesus," he continued, "fulfills all the hopes and expectations of the Jewish people."[195]

The second multiplication miracle took place in Decapolis. The Decapolis, as noted in Father Callam's article, was "in the region of the ten cities east of the Jordan River." He further noted that "the people fed were Gentiles." There were seven loaves used for this miracle, which Father Callam stated, "signifies completion or perfection, as in the seven days of creation or the seven gifts of the Holy Spirit." There were seven baskets of leftovers, which implied that "there was enough bread for future feeding of all the Gentiles." In his article, Father Callam stated that "all the Gentiles had not yet been invited to the Messianic banquet." "But they will be," he continued, "once the Apostles 'make disciples of all nations.'"[196]

Father Callam ended his article by focusing on another important number. That number was number one. In the Gospel of Mark, immediately following the feeding of the 4,000, Jesus got into a boat with his disciples. Scripture stated that "they had forgotten to bring bread, and they had only one loaf with them in the boat."[197] "We know from Saint Paul," wrote Father Callam, "that the single loaf is symbolic of the Eucharist and of our being members of Christ's Mystical Body." In the New Testament, we read, "Because the loaf of bread is one, we, though many, are one body, for we all partake of the one loaf."[198] Father Callam stated that "it is clear, therefore, that the multiplication of the loaves foreshadows the Eucharist." He further concluded that no matter how "fragmented the loaves may be, there is unity in the Church because of the one loaf, one bread of the Eucharist."[199] This was a powerful statement, especially as we encounter much fragmentation in our world today in both politics and religion. No matter how fragmented the loaves may be, there will always be unity in the Church. There was only one loaf. There was only one Eucharist. As noted in the *Catechism of the Catholic Church*, the miracles of the multiplication of the loaves "prefigures the superabundance of this unique bread of His Eucharist."[200] God makes Himself available in the Eucharist. There will always be a superabundance of His Body, Blood, Soul, and Divinity in the Eucharist for all of us.

Reflection

As I reflect further on this Eighth Station of the Eucharist, I consider one of the most important characters in the story – the young boy with the five loaves and two fish. I place myself in the scene as this young boy who is headed home from the market after purchasing the items his mother requested.

As I walk home with my basket securely fastened around my waist, I notice a crowd forming. I am curious and move toward them. I recognize Peter and the other disciples. I can also see Jesus. I have never met him before, but others have told me about Him. Jesus is talking with several of His disciples when suddenly, Andrew says, "There is a boy here who has five barley loaves and two fish." He is pointing directly at me as he says this. My eyes widen with unbelief. These are the items for my family. Andrew then shrugs, looks at Jesus, and says, "What good are these for so many?" I couldn't agree more. Besides, it would not be a good idea to go home empty-handed. Jesus then gives instructions for the crowd to recline. As I peer out over the massive crowd, I know that Jesus must have a better plan than what I have in my basket.

Suddenly, Jesus motions for me to come closer. I am afraid to do so. I need to bring this food home to my family. I can feel Andrew's hand on my back as he moves me closer to Jesus. Jesus then gazes at me with a peaceful smile and loving eyes. He reaches into my basket and takes the loaves. As He begins to pray, I bow my head in prayer. However, there is a different prayer in my heart. I do not have any more money to purchase additional bread for my family. I have younger siblings who depend on me. My father works hard every day in the field. If I do not bring home the items my mother requested, my father will have nothing to eat when he returns home.

As I raise my head, I can see people shuffling all around me. The bread and fish are being broken repeatedly. It keeps multiplying until everyone is fed. Suddenly, there are twelve baskets that have come forward. When I peer inside one of the baskets, it is full of bread and fish. I look inside another and see the same thing. All twelve baskets are full of bread and fish. As I glance back up at the crowd, many are still eating. I then look up at Jesus with both my mouth and eyes open wide. I wonder – *How did He do this?* Jesus has the same peaceful expression on His face as before. His eyes portray the kind of love that I have seen in my mother's eyes as she watches our family eat one of her favorite meals. I can tell as I stand next to Jesus that He knew what He was going to do. He is not at all concerned with the number of people who need to be fed. He also is not limited by the little that I brought forward.

As I watch this miracle unfold, I think of Abraham and his wife, Sarah. I heard the story of Abraham and Sarah from my parents and my rabbi. All Jews know this story. Abraham and Sarah were an elderly couple who had no children. Yet God said to Abraham, "I will make your descendants as numerous as the stars in the sky."[201] *How could this happen when they are both old and beyond childbearing years?* It is the same question I wonder about this miracle. *How can you feed this massive crowd with the small amount of food that I have in my basket?* God does not seem to be limited by the quantity that we bring before Him. With faith and trust in Him, He uses the small amounts brought to Him to accomplish His purpose. From Abraham and Sarah, my entire village exists. All the people before me, eating from the little that I brought, are descendants of Abraham and Sarah.

It was difficult to give what was in my basket to Jesus. I did not want to give it. But all eyes were on me, and I felt compelled to do so. I realize now that all that I have in the hands of Jesus can be used for good. Not only has the entire crowd been fed, but I can now bring food to my family. With all the leftovers, I can bring more than what was requested by my mother.

The crowd realizes the miracle as well. They do not want Jesus to leave. They talk among themselves, saying that He is *truly the Prophet, the one who is to come into the world.* Jesus seems to know what they are thinking. He motions to His disciples, indicating that He will be leaving. He pats me on the head and walks away from the crowd toward the mountain.

The crowd begins to disperse. My basket is now full of leftovers from this amazing event. As I make my way toward my home, I can see several people from the crowd talking to my mother. My mother looks up at me and waits as I come closer. With tears in my eyes, I open the basket for my mother to see what has been given. She is speechless, and her eyes swell with tears as she sees before her enough food to feed her family for the next week. We hug each other still trying to comprehend all that has occurred. My mother takes the basket from me and moves quickly toward our home. I look toward the field and can see my father working on the land. Several men from the crowd are talking with him about the events of the day. Suddenly, my father and I make eye contact. He raises his hand toward me to greet me. I do the same. Despite the distance, I can see a glisten in his eyes. This miracle has touched my father, and he seems relieved for his family.

I have learned so much today about this man named Jesus. I know in my heart that He is the Messiah, and I am very glad to have met Him. I will not hesitate, from this point forward, to give Him all that I have, no matter how little it may be.

++++++++++

Prayerfully consider the young boy in this miracle. All of us have been given talents and gifts. Sometimes, we consider our gifts too small to make a difference. Because of this multiplication miracle, prayerfully consider trusting God with all your resources. List all your gifts and talents, and allow Jesus to multiply your resources in ways you could have never imagined.

PRAYER NOTES

PRAYER NOTES

Chapter 9

The Bread of Life Discourse

Chapter 9

The Bread of Life Discourse

The Bread of Life Discourse is the Ninth Station of the Eucharist. This controversial discourse can be found in the sixth chapter of the Gospel of John. From the moment Jesus spoke these words, there has been controversy and opinions that have led many down different roads. Let's dive into this exciting chapter in John's Gospel and discover the truth about the Eucharist.

Chapter six in the Gospel of John began with the multiplication miracle of the five barley loaves and two fish. The crowd of 5,000 was so impressed with this miracle that they concluded among themselves that Jesus was "the Prophet, the one who is to come into the world."[202] The crowd wanted to carry Jesus away and make Him king. Jesus knew this and "withdrew again to the mountain alone."[203] Although the Gospel of John did not indicate what Jesus did on the mountain, the Gospel of Mark was clear. Immediately following the multiplication miracle noted in the Gospel of Mark, it stated that "when he [Jesus] had taken leave of them, he went off to the mountain to pray."[204]

Prayer is very important in life. In an article by *Catholic Daily Reflections*, it stated that the "mountain is a symbol of our journey toward God." It further stated that "the mountain that we are called to go up is first and foremost prayer." Prayer should occur daily in our lives. "Unless we go up that mountain," the article concluded, "we will be ill-equipped to fulfill His divine commission. We will be insufficiently prepared to bring His love and mercy to a world in need."[205]

An article by David Platt stated that "Jesus prioritized time with His heavenly Father." Jesus went to the mountain to be with His Father upon realizing that the crowd wanted to make Him king. Platt stated that Jesus knew "that God had not called Him to be king in this way." "Jesus knew," according to Platt, "that the Father was calling Him to become king in a very different way, a way that would lead to a cruel death on a cross." It was for this reason, Platt concluded, that "He goes aside to be with the Father." In reflection, Platt also shared that "there are all kinds of pursuits this world may put before you that are not from God." "It takes discipline," he said, "to come aside and be with God."[206] An article by Terry Storch stated that "Jesus knew that the worldly praise that was coming from the crowds would bring no real fuel for his soul." Storch stated that Jesus "retreated and withdrew to spend time with the Father, the only one who can truly fill our soul."[207]

Scripture does not speak to the whereabouts of the disciples once Jesus left for the mountain. Perhaps they were assisting the crowd in their departure. Or maybe they were distributing the food from the twelve leftover baskets. Scripture is clear to note, however, that "when it was evening, his disciples went down to the sea, embarked in a boat, and went across the sea to Capernaum."[208] During their journey across the sea, the disciples experienced a strong wind. As they pursued the task of rowing against the wind, "they saw Jesus walking on the sea and coming near the boat, and they began to be afraid."[209] Obviously, this was not what they expected. I can imagine the rowing ceased as they each strained to see Jesus on the water. Perhaps they wondered how this was possible. I am sure these were the same thoughts they had when witnessing the multiplication of the loaves and fish earlier in the day. Despite their fear, Scripture tells us that "they wanted to take him [Jesus] into the boat, but the boat immediately arrived at the shore to which they were heading."[210]

Again, Scripture does not tell us what happened that evening after the boat arrived on shore. However, the next day, the crowd that witnessed the multiplication miracle was in search of Jesus. Noticing that only one boat remained at their shore, they concluded that Jesus sailed with His disciples to Capernaum. Before long, many boats carrying large numbers of people sailed to Capernaum searching for Jesus. When they finally found Jesus, a conversation occurred between Jesus and the people who had searched for Him.

> *They said to him, "Rabbi, when did you get here?" Jesus answered them and said, "Amen Amen, I say to you, you are looking for me not because you saw signs but because you ate the loaves and were filled. Do not work for food that perishes but for the food that endures for eternal life, which the Son of Man will give you. For on him the Father, God, has set his seal." So they said to him, "What can we do to accomplish the works of God?" Jesus answered and said to them, "This is the work of God, that you believe in the one he sent." So they said to him, "What sign can you do, that we may see and believe in you?"* **John 6:25-30**

It was mind-boggling that the crowd that witnessed the multiplication miracle the day prior would ask Jesus for another sign. However, forgetting about the miracle that occurred the day before, they referred to the manna that was provided to their ancestors in the desert.

> *"Our ancestors ate manna in the desert, as it is written: 'He gave them bread from heaven to eat.'"* **John 6:31**

The conversation continued,

> *So Jesus said to them, "Amen, amen, I say to you, it was not Moses who gave the bread from heaven; my Father gives you the true bread from heaven. For the bread of God is that which comes down from heaven and gives life to the world." So they said to him, "Sir, give us this bread always."*
>
> *Jesus said to them, "I am the bread of life; whoever comes to me will never hunger, and whoever believes in me will never thirst. But I told you that although you have seen me, you do not believe. Everything that the Father gives me will come to me, and I will not reject anyone who comes to me, because I came down from heaven not to do my own will but the will of the one who sent me. And this is the will of the one who sent me, that I should not lose anything of what he gave me, but that I should raise it on the last day. For this is the will of my Father, that everyone who sees the Son and believes in him may have eternal life, and I shall raise him on the last day."* **John 6: 32-40**

The Jews began to murmur among themselves. They were trying to figure out what Jesus' words meant. They did not understand how He could say that He was "the bread that came down from heaven," when they knew his parents. He was no one special to them. Yet, this familiar person, the day prior, performed an amazing miracle that fed 5,000 people with only five loaves and two fish.

Finally, Jesus said to them,

> *"Stop your murmuring among yourselves. No one can come to me unless the Father who sent me draw him, and I will raise him on the last day. It is written in the prophets: 'They shall all be taught by God.' Everyone who listens to my Father and learns from him comes to me. Not that anyone has seen the Father except the one who is from God; he has seen the Father. Amen, amen, I say to you, whoever believes has eternal life. I am the bread of life."* **John 6:43-48**

Jesus then addressed their concern for the manna provided to their ancestors in the desert.

> *"Your ancestors ate the manna in the desert, but they died; this is the bread that comes down from heaven so that one may eat it and not die."* **John 6:49-50**

Jesus had their undivided attention. No one wants to experience death. This Jesus, who they thought they knew, was about to tell them how they could avoid death. Jesus continued,

> *"I am the living bread that came down from heaven; whoever eats this bread will live forever, and the bread that I will give is my flesh for the life of the world."* **John 6:51**

As these words were being shared, I am sure many of them thought, "That's it, I'm out of here!" Maybe at that moment, people did not physically leave, but their minds shut off to the possibility of Jesus giving them his flesh as bread. People began quarreling among themselves as they tried to make sense of Jesus' words. Many may have wondered, "What are we supposed to do with his flesh?" Jesus then continued with an explanation.

> *"Amen, amen, I say to you, unless you eat the flesh of the Son of Man and drink his blood, you do not have life within you."* **John 6:53**

Flesh <u>AND</u> blood! I am sure many of them at this point at least thought to themselves that this was more than they could handle. Yet Jesus continued,

> *"Whoever eats my flesh and drinks my blood has eternal life and I will raise him on the last day. For my flesh is true food, and my blood is true drink. Whoever eats my flesh and drinks my blood remains in me and I in him. Just as the living Father sent me and I have life because of the Father, so also the one who feeds on me will have life because of me. This is the bread that came down from heaven. Unlike your ancestors who ate and still died, whoever eats this bread will live forever."* **John 6:54-59**

This was an amazing discourse. Jesus spoke with authority. He was very serious about what He shared. The crowd that He spoke to in the Gospel of John was shocked by His words. Many of them threw up their hands in disgust and walked away.

Reflection

As I reflect on this station, I place myself in the scene as a member of the crowd. I have a young family. My wife and two small children are at home. I have spent my life in the synagogue, learning from respectable rabbis. Many of the elders of my synagogue are with me as we listen to Jesus' words. We are determined to find Jesus and travel by boat to see Him. Yesterday was another unusual day when Jesus took a small amount of bread and fish and fed 5,000. I was standing close to the young boy who provided the small meal. I witnessed the blessing provided by Jesus and saw everyone being fed. When it was my turn to receive the food, I put out my hand in unbelief. The man distributing the food gave me a small loaf of bread and a fish. I could not believe my eyes. As I ate the meal, twelve baskets came forward, filled to the rim with leftover food. I do not know how this miracle was possible. For this reason, I knew I wanted to join the others in finding Jesus.

I have listened to the conversation between the elders and Jesus, and like those with me, I, too, am shocked at Jesus' proposal to eat His flesh and drink His blood. Many men from my synagogue have walked away. As the people leave in droves, I expect Jesus to say something. But He is silent. He offers no explanation for the unusual words He proclaimed. Instead, He turns to His apostles and began speaking with them. I move in closer to listen to what is being said.

"Do you also want to leave?" Jesus asks His close friends.[211] This is a direct question. The apostles squirm as they try to figure out how to respond. Suddenly, Peter, who I met the day before during the distribution of the loaves and fish, comes forward. With boldness, Peter says, "Master, to whom shall we go? You have the words of eternal life. We have come to believe and are convinced that you are the Holy One of God."[212] I am not as convinced as Peter, but his words are compelling. Jesus then responds to them, "Did I not choose you twelve? Yet is not one of you a devil?"[213] My eyes widen with concern. Jesus seems to know the hearts and thoughts of those close to Him. I decide to leave before He has a chance to read my thoughts.

As I walk toward the shore, I think about all that has occurred. Once at the seashore, I see one of my neighbors boarding a boat. I quickly approach and ask if there is room for one more. I am invited to join them. As we make our way home across the sea, my mind is filled with wonder as I remember the multiplication miracle from the day before. I do not know how that miracle occurred. But it did, and I witnessed it all. I then think of the other miracles taught by our rabbis from many years ago. The miracle of Abraham and Sarah having a child in their old age does not make sense, yet it happened, and we are all here because of that miracle. The miracle of the burning bush was one I grappled with as a young child. How can a bush be engulfed in flames but not burn? Yet we know it occurred. The Torah clearly shares Moses' experience with the burning bush. Somehow, I feel the importance of faith is needed to fully understand Jesus' words regarding His flesh and blood.

Once home, I sit near the fire and spend time with my children and wife. As laughter and joy fill my home, my mind still thinks about Jesus and His unusual words. I wonder if I will ever see Him again and how His words will impact my family.

++++++++++

Prayerfully consider the importance of faith in understanding Jesus' words. Do you struggle with the true presence of Our Lord in the Eucharist? Do you wonder how the God of the universe can be presented to you in the form of bread and wine?

Can you explain the miracle of the burning bush without faith? Can you explain the birth of Isaac to Abraham and Sarah in their old age? The same miracle took place in Saint Elizabeth with the birth of John the Baptist. Do you recall instances in your life that made you look to God for answers, or did you consider the instances mere coincidences? Because of God's greatness, faith is necessary to accept all that He has accomplished for us and continues to do in our lives. With the eyes of faith, consider again the words of Jesus in the sixth chapter of the Gospel of John.

> *"Unless you eat the flesh of the Son of Man and drink his blood, you do not have life within you. Whoever eats my flesh and drinks my blood has eternal life, and I will raise him on the last day. For my flesh is true food, and my blood is true drink. Whoever eats my flesh and drinks my blood remains in me and I in him."* **John 6:53-56**

This is the Ninth Station of the Eucharist. There are three more stations that will provide a deeper understanding of the true presence of Our Lord and Savior in the Eucharist. Before moving on to the next chapter, spend time with Our Lord, sharing with Him all that you have learned so far in this journey through the Stations of the Eucharist.

PRAYER NOTES

PRAYER NOTES

Chapter 10

The Last Supper

Chapter 10

The Last Supper

The Bread of Life Discourse, discussed in the previous chapter, can sometimes be watered down to mere symbolism or figurative language. An article by *Catholic Life Journal* stated that the 2019 Pew Research Center survey "found that 69% of Catholics believe bread and wine are symbols, while only 31% of Catholics believe the Church's teaching around transubstantiation."[214] A new study, however, by Vinea Research has found that "69% of Mass-going Catholics believe in the real presence of Jesus in the Eucharist." This study suggested that "more than two-thirds of Catholics believe the Eucharist is truly Jesus."[215]

The term *transubstantiation*, according to an article by Francis J. Ripley, stated that it was "first used by Hildebert of Tours around 1079." The term *transubstantiation*, as noted in the *Catechism of the Catholic Church*, was used in the Council of Trent (between 1545 and 1563) to summarize the Catholic faith. The Council summary stated,

> *Because Christ our Redeemer said that it was truly his body that he was offering under the species of bread, it has always been the conviction of the Church of God, and this holy Council now declares again, that by the consecration of the bread and wine there takes place a change of the whole substance of the bread into the substance of the body of Christ our Lord and of the whole substance of the wine into the substance of his blood. This change the holy Catholic Church has fittingly and properly called transubstantiation.* **CCC 1376**

Ripley further stated that "the dogmas of Christ's Real Presence in the Eucharist remained unmolested down to the ninth century."[216] Ripley's article shared several New Testament Scriptures written by Saint Paul that confirmed the tradition and meaning of what occurred at the Last Supper.

The Last Supper is the Tenth Station of the Eucharist. This event was noted in the Gospels of Matthew, Mark, and Luke. The supper took place on the feast of Unleavened Bread. This was the day for sacrificing the Passover lamb. The apostles asked Jesus, "Where do you want us to prepare for you to eat the Passover?"[217] Jesus gave specific instructions to two of the apostles on where to go, who they would meet, and what they were to say. In the Gospel of Luke, it was noted that the two apostles sent to prepare for this meal were Peter and John. The instructions were followed, and the preparations were made. Jesus then took His place at the table with the apostles. Jesus began by saying,

> *"I have eagerly desired to eat this Passover with you before I suffer, for, I tell you, I shall not eat it (again) until there is fulfillment in the kingdom of God."* **Luke 22:15-16**

This was an odd way to begin the Passover meal. Before the apostles considered what was being said, Jesus took a cup, gave thanks, and said,

> *"Take this and share it among yourselves; for I tell you that from this time on I shall not drink of the fruit of the vine until the kingdom of God comes."* **Luke 22:17-18**

Perhaps the apostles were excited to hear Jesus speak about the kingdom of God. However, these were not the usual words spoken on Passover. Jesus then began the traditional Passover meal by taking bread. He said the blessing and broke the bread. This was familiar to the apostles; however, as the bread was being distributed to those around the table, Jesus said,

> *"This is my body, which will be given for you; do this in memory of me."* **Luke 22:19**

Never has any rabbi said similar words while distributing the bread at Passover. These were strange words, yet it might be possible that some, if not all the apostles, reflected on the Bread of Life Discourse spoken by Jesus days earlier during the multiplication miracle. At that time, Jesus clearly said, "The bread that I will give you is my flesh for the life of the world."[218] Perhaps the apostles were connecting the dots. Jesus had taken bread at this special meal and said clearly while referring to the bread and distributing to those at table, *"This is my body."*[219] In addition, the apostles also understood that this was something Jesus wanted them to do in memory of him.

After the bread was consumed, Jesus then took the cup and said,

> *"This cup is the new covenant in my blood, which will be shed for you."* **Luke 22:20**

Again, the words of the Bread of Life Discourse might have been recalled in the hearts and minds of the apostles. In this discourse, Jesus said, "Unless you eat the flesh of the Son of Man and drink his blood, you do not have life within you. Whoever eats my flesh and drinks my blood has eternal life, and I will raise him on the last day. For my flesh is true food, and my blood is true drink. Whoever eats my flesh and drinks my blood remains in me and I in him."[220]

The word *covenant* might also have had a profound impact on the apostles. The *Catholic Encyclopedia* defined covenant as "a solemn promise, fortified by an oath, concerning future action."[221] "Most scholars," according to an article by Catholic Answers, "recognize five major covenants in the Bible." These included the covenants made between God and Noah, Abraham, Moses, and David. "The New Covenant," as noted in this article was, "established through the prophet Jeremiah and fulfilled in Jesus." This new covenant "does away with the legal requirements of commandments and replaces them with a desire of the heart to do the will of God." The article further stated that this "covenant is with all humanity."[222]

The apostles were familiar with the covenants of Noah, Abraham, Moses, and David. However, this new covenant required a shift in their thinking. As they pondered the meaning of Jesus' words regarding His body and blood, they might have also wondered about the commission provided by Jesus to "do this in memory of me."[223]

Ripley's article on *transubstantiation* as noted earlier, also addressed the first epistle to the Corinthians written by Saint Paul. "First Corinthians," Ripley said, "was written after the Passover of 57…or 27 years after Christ's death." "This means," Ripley stated, "the newly converted Saul, now Paul, was plunged into the infant Church as early as four and not later than seven years after the death of Christ." "He was," Ripley pointed out, "an eyewitness of the earliest Eucharistic celebrations or liturgical practices." In addressing the Corinthians in his first letter, Paul wrote,

> *For I received from the Lord what I also handed on to you, that the Lord Jesus, on the night he was handed over, took bread, and, after he had given*

thanks, broke it and said, "This is my body that is for you. Do this in remembrance of me." In the same way also the cup, after supper, saying, "This cup is the new covenant in my blood. Do this, as often as you drink it, in remembrance of me." **1 Corinthians 11:23-25**

In Chapter 10 of the first letter of Saint Paul to the Corinthians, Saint Paul asked two questions.

The cup of blessing that we bless, is it not a participation in the blood of Christ? The bread that we break, is it not a participation in the body of Christ? **1 Corinthians 10:16**

"The only possible meaning," according to Ripley, was that "the bread and wine at the consecration become Christ's actual body and blood." "Evidently," Ripley continued, "Paul believed that the words Christ had said at the Last Supper...meant that really and physically the bread is his body." "In fact," he continued, "Christ was not merely saying that the bread was his body; he was decreeing that it should be so and that it is so."[224]

Saint Paul made it clear in his letter to the Galatians that,

The gospel preached by me is not of human origin. For I did not receive it from a human being, nor was I taught it, but it came through a revelation of Jesus Christ. **Galatians 1:11-12**

In addition, Saint Paul encouraged the Philippians to,

Keep on doing what you have learned and received and heard and seen in me. **Philippians 4:9**

Saint Paul was handing down a tradition that comes from Christ. In his second letter to the Thessalonians, Paul wrote,

> *God chose you as the firstfruits for salvation through sanctification by the Spirit and belief in truth. To this end, he has also called you through our gospel to possess the glory of our Lord Jesus Christ. Therefore, brothers, stand firm and hold fast to the traditions that you were taught, either by an oral statement or by a letter of ours.* **2 Thessalonians 2:13-15**

Despite the consistency in Scripture of the Real Presence of Christ in the Eucharist, it was not until the ninth century that controversy became prevalent regarding the truth of the Eucharist. The Council of Trent, between 1545 and 1563, as noted in the *Catechism of the Catholic Church* and stated earlier in this writing, addressed the controversy and confirmed the truths of the Eucharist.

The United States Council of Catholic Bishops (USCCB) stated that the term *Eucharist* "originates from the Greek word *eucharistia*, meaning thanksgiving." The USCCB also stated that "the presence of Christ in the Eucharist is real, true, and substantial." The Eucharistic prayer, as noted by the USCCB, "is the heart of the Liturgy of the Eucharist." The USCCB further stated that "in this prayer, the celebrant acts in the person of Christ as head of his body, the Church. He [Christ] gathers not only the bread and the wine, but the substance of our lives and joins them to Christ's perfect sacrifice, offering them to the Father."[225]

Reflection

The Real Presence of Jesus in the Eucharist may be difficult for us to consider. It is truly impossible to understand without faith. One way that we can better understand this station is by accepting the challenge of Saint Ignatius of Loyola to place ourselves at the scene.

When the crowds dispersed after Jesus' words about eating His flesh and drinking His blood, Jesus turned to the apostles and asked them if they wanted to leave, too. It was Peter who spoke for the apostles. He said clearly, "Master, to whom shall we go? You have the words of eternal life. We have come to believe and are convinced that you are the Holy One of God."[226]

Peter spoke with faith. It was with faith that Peter led the Church. He encouraged us to walk in faith and to see the things of God through the eyes of faith.

In this reflection, I choose the role of Peter as I consider the details of this station and the events surrounding it.

As it gets closer to Passover, I am more aware of the grumbling of the chief priests and scribes. They seem determined to do harm to Jesus. I want to protect Jesus. I cannot imagine what life would be like without him. As I accompany the others through the market area, I notice Judas walking toward the temple. I decide to follow him. There is something about Judas that makes me question his loyalty to Jesus. From a distance, I see him talking with the chief priests and temple guards. I am too far away to hear what they are saying. But I take note of the situation and hope to have an opportunity later to confront Judas about his conversation with them.

I catch up with the others. I make eye contact with Jesus, who then assigns John and me to make the preparations for the Passover meal. John and I have prepared for the Passover many times before. However, this time, we are not sure where Jesus would like to have this meal. There are a few options that I can think of. Certainly, my home is available, if that is what Jesus wants. John then asks Jesus, "Where do you want us to make the preparations?" Jesus then gives us detailed instructions. I listen intently and then John and I set out toward the city. As we begin the journey, I lean toward John and ask, "Did you get all that?" John immediately responds, "Yeah, I think so." He then begins to repeat the instructions Jesus has given. "Once we get into the city," John says, "we will meet a man carrying a jar of water."[227] My eyes widen and I think to myself how odd this would be. Women are the ones that supply the water. We see them throughout our towns carrying water from the wells for their homes and families. A man carrying the water is an odd thing to see. We should not have any problem identifying him. I glance at John as we move toward the city. John continues with the instructions. "Once we find this man, we are to follow him into the house that he enters. Then we are instructed to speak to the master of the house about the availability of the guest room for the Passover meal."

As we continue our walk, John then says, "I keep repeating Jesus' words in my head. I don't want to get this wrong. When we see the master of the house, we are to say – *'the teacher says to you, where is the guest room where I may eat the Passover with my disciples?'*"[228] John shrugs and says, "Maybe we will recognize the master of this house as one of the followers of Jesus." I have no idea how this will play out, but I have been with Jesus long enough to trust what He says.

Once inside the city, our eyes canvass the area. There are many people in every direction. People are busy buying and selling items. As expected, women are carrying water jars. However, we see one man, as Jesus said, with a water jar. We know this is the man to follow.

After a few yards, the man enters a house. There is nothing special about the house. It is a simple home with basic furnishings. Upon entering the home, we notice a kitchen to the left and can see a woman preparing vegetables. The man with the water jar goes toward the kitchen. My eyes immediately move to the right of the home, where I see a man sitting at a large desk. I tap John's arm. John then glances in my direction. Once he sees the man, John approaches him. The man stops what he is doing and makes eye contact with John. John then repeats Jesus' words, *"The teacher says to you, 'Where is the guest room where I may eat the Passover with my disciples?'"* The man smiles at John and then looks toward me. He then stands up and walks around his desk toward John. He greets John with a warm embrace and says with joy, "Welcome." He then walks toward me and does the same. I do not recognize this man, and from the expression on John's face, neither does he. But the welcome is warm and genuine, and we know we are in the right place. The man then says, "Follow me." We walk toward the back of the home, where a large room is available. The man then says, "You can celebrate the Passover meal here." He then adds, "My servants and I are available to help you in any way."

With the generous help of this man and his servants, we prepare the guest room for the Passover meal. The ingredients for the sacred meal, including the lamb and unleavened bread, are prepared by the kitchen servants. There are several jugs of wine offered by the owner of the home for our celebration. To ensure we will not run out of wine, John and I purchase several jugs of wine at the local market. When we arrive back at the home, we enter the guest room and carefully observe the surroundings to ensure everything was in its place. The table in the center of the room is about 18 inches off the ground, with several beautiful pillows at each setting. Reclining at the table is an important part of this celebration. On the table are all the necessary items beautifully displayed. At each place setting, there are four glasses for the ritual wine. One plate, cutlery, and a napkin are also displayed at each setting. In the center of the table, there are several candles.[229]

From the time I was a child, Passover was always a special celebration. Things were done with precision to include assigned seating. The head of the family always had a special place at the table. The guests would then wrap around the table on either side of this special place of honor from the oldest to the youngest or the most important to the least important.[230] I know that at this Passover, Jesus will be given the special place of honor.

The smell of the roasted lamb permeates the air and is a reminder of the celebration that will take place. As I enter the kitchen, I can see all the food prepared for this event. The *charoset*, pronounced *har-o-set*, is one of my favorite flavors of Passover. In Hebrew, the word means *clay*. The *charoset* is a sweet relish made with fruits, nuts, spices, as well as wine and honey.[231] The *charoset* mixture is placed on the seder plate and symbolizes the mortar the Israelites used to build storehouses for Pharaoh.[232] In addition to the *charoset*, there are baskets of unleavened bread, vegetables, and a jar of vinegar on the kitchen table. All these items will be placed on the Passover table in the designated room once the guests begin arriving.

Everything is in its place, including the area near the front door where the servants will wash the feet of those entering the home. A small table is also placed near the entrance to the home. Upon it are several wine glasses and bottles of non-ritual wine. This will be given to the guests after the servants wash their feet. One by one, the guests will then be escorted to the table.

As we wait patiently for Jesus and the other apostles to arrive, we talk among ourselves with the owner of the home and his servants. Suddenly, a young boy with great joy comes to the front door and announces, "They're coming!" Upon hearing this, the kitchen servants bring the first course of food to the table. This includes the *charoset,* unleavened bread, vegetables, and vinegar.

Jesus is the first to enter the home. I am so happy to see Him. We embrace with great joy. One by one, our friends arrive. It is so good to see all of them. The servants begin washing their feet. John and I then hand each of them a glass of wine and, one by one, escort them to the Passover table. Once we are all seated, Jesus begins with an unusual statement. "I have eagerly desired to eat this Passover with you before I suffer, for, I tell you, I shall not eat it again until there is fulfillment in the kingdom of God."[233] Somehow, I know that this will be a very different Passover celebration. I watch intently as Jesus takes a piece of the unleavened bread. After providing the blessing, He breaks the bread and shares it with us. While doing so, He says, "This is my body, which will be given for you; do this in memory of me."[234] My mind immediately goes back to the words Jesus spoke after the multiplication miracle. At that time, He said, "I am the living bread that came down from heaven; whoever eats this bread will live forever; and the bread that I will give is my flesh for the life of the world."[235] I am beginning to see the connection. I also recognize the importance of this bread and a sense of urgency to share its truth with others.

Jesus does not rush the prayer. He waits until each of us receives the bread which He states clearly is His body. I am sitting next to John when he hands me the bread. I take a piece and pass it to James, who is sitting next to me. I look at the bread, and I reflect on the words Jesus said, "This is my body." I reverently place the bread in my mouth. How is it, I wonder, that the Messiah I have longed for all my life is now resting on my tongue? What Jesus is saying to all of us is that He wants us to consume Him. He is the nourishment we need for the journey to eternity. This is like the manna that nourished our ancestors who traveled to the Promised Land. However, this bread is so much better. It is, as Jesus says, His body, and He is the long awaited Messiah. As I consume the bread, I make eye contact with Jesus. With a gentle smile of love and a nod, Jesus continues by taking the cup that has been filled with the ritual Passover wine. He then raises the cup before us and says, "This cup is the new covenant in my blood, which will be shed for you."[236]

I cringe every time Jesus talks about suffering. I do not want to see Him suffer. I do not understand why that is necessary. Yet, at the Passover meal, I understand the importance of the blood that was shed by the lamb. If the lamb's blood was not placed on the lintels of the homes of the Israelites, their firstborn would have died as God declared. Jesus is now giving us this ritual

Passover wine and telling us that it is His blood. He further states that His blood must be shed for us. In essence, He is telling us that He is our sacrificial lamb. I really wish this could be played out differently; however, He seems determined. I receive the cup from John, take a sip, and then pass it to James. I know I am frowning with great concern. However, Jesus is at peace and is committed to what He knows He must do.

++++++++++

Jesus' words in both the Eighth and Ninth Stations of the Eucharist make it clear that the bread He offers to us is, in fact, His Body, Blood, Soul, and Divinity. He provides Himself to us in this special meal. Take a few moments to share with Our Lord your thoughts upon receiving Him in the Eucharist. How do you prepare for this special encounter? What are your thoughts as Jesus is placed on your tongue? What are your expectations after receiving the Eucharist? Do you see a connection between receiving the Eucharist and being sent into the world to share the good news?

PRAYER NOTES

PRAYER NOTES

Chapter 11

The Road to Emmaus

Chapter 11

The Road to Emmaus

The Eleventh Station of the Eucharist is also noted as one of the Stations of the Resurrection. I had an opportunity to research this station for my book *The Way of Light: The Story Behind the Stations of the Resurrection*. However, to prepare for this writing, I decided to look deeper and begin with what occurred prior to the Road to Emmaus experience.

Following the crucifixion, Joseph of Arimathea received permission from Pilate to take Jesus' body for burial. The Gospel of John further states that "Nicodemus, the one who had first come to him at night, also came bringing a mixture of myrrh and aloes weighing about one hundred pounds."[237] It is also noted in the Gospel of John that standing at the foot of the cross of Jesus prior to his death were "his mother and his mother's sister, Mary the wife of Clopas, and Mary of Magdala." The apostle John was also present and the only apostle who did not abandon Jesus. Jesus spoke to His mother and the apostle John before dying on the cross.[238]

After Jesus' death, Joseph of Arimathea and Nicodemus removed the body of Jesus from the cross and prepared it for burial. This was a daunting task that required the support of more than two men. In the Gospel of John, we learn that immediately after the crucifixion, the soldiers "took his clothes and divided them into four shares, a share for each soldier."[239] There were at least four soldiers who assisted in the crucifixion. If it took four soldiers to place Jesus on the cross, it was highly unlikely that it took only two men to take Him down. In addition, Scripture clearly stated that Nicodemus brought one hundred pounds of myrrh and aloe for the burial. Did Nicodemus carry this himself or did he have assistance from others? An article by Byron R. McCane stated that "according to third-century C.E. Jewish tractate *Semahot*, men could only prepare the corpse of a man, but women could prepare both men and women."[240] Knowing that Jesus' mother, Saint John, Mary Magdalene, and the other women were at the crucifixion, I believe that they were also present at the burial, which took place shortly after Jesus' death. Joseph of Arimathea's request for Jesus' body was not only to ensure he received a proper burial. But also to ensure that the burial took place before the Sabbath. The Gospels all agree that Jesus died on a Friday, a few hours before the Jewish Sabbath was to begin.[241] A detailed description of the preparation of Jesus' body for burial was provided in the writings of Saint Anne Catherine Emmerich. Saint Emmerich shares that, in her visions, after removing Jesus' body from the cross, "the men laid the Sacred Body on a sheet spread upon the Mother's lap. The adorable head of Jesus rested upon her slightly raised knee, and His body lay outstretched upon the sheet." Saint Emmerich further stated that as the Blessed Mother "pressed her lips to His blood-stained cheeks…Magdalene knelt with her face bowed upon His feet."[242]

Despite the one hundred pounds of myrrh and aloes used to prepare Jesus' body for burial, Mary Magdalene and the other women "returned and prepared spices and perfumed oils. They then rested on the Sabbath according to the commandment." However, "at the daybreak of the first day of the week, they took the spices they had prepared and went to the tomb."[243] Research on the significance of the spices used indicated that "the main reason a dead body was anointed with spices was to control the smell of decomposition." An article on this topic also stated that "the fact that the women brought spices to anoint

Jesus' dead body showed they did not expect Jesus to literally rise from the dead."[244] As Mary Magdalene and the other women approached the tomb, they might have wondered how they would remove the stone to apply the spices to Jesus' body. As they approached the tomb, they noticed the stone was not in its proper place. When they entered the tomb, "They did not find the body of the Lord Jesus."[245]

Scripture tells us further that while the women "were puzzling over this, behold, two men in dazzling garments appeared to them. They were terrified and bowed their faces to the ground." The men then said to them, "Why do you seek the living one among the dead? He is not here, but he has been raised. Remember what he said to you while he was still in Galilee, that the Son of Man must be handed over to sinners and be crucified and rise on the third day." Upon hearing this, the women remembered Jesus' words. With great joy, Mary Magdalene and the other women returned from the tomb and announced all these things to the eleven remaining apostles and to all the others.[246]

The two men featured in this Station of the Eucharist were part of the assembly that heard the proclamation of Mary Magdalene and the other women. The Gospel of Luke tells us that the women's story "seemed like nonsense, and they did not believe them." However, "Peter got up and ran to the tomb, bent down, and saw the burial cloths alone; then he went home amazed at what had happened."[247] No one had an explanation for what was seen by the women. Peter was also silent in explaining what occurred. The people were confused and not sure what to believe.

One of the men in the assembly was named Cleopas. With all the confusion and uncertainty, perhaps he decided that it was time to go home. As he set out, another disciple joined him. These men were quite troubled. They wanted to believe but they also did not want to be foolish in their thinking. With their heads bowed low and their hearts saddened by all that had occurred, they headed home to Emmaus. It was approximately seven miles from Jerusalem to Emmaus. These men had recently come to Jerusalem to celebrate Passover. So much had occurred since they arrived. Despite their lack of understanding, the men decided to go home. But what exactly were they going home to? Without an explanation of what had occurred, were they planning to go back to living as if the recent events did not happen?

While these two men were traveling home to Emmaus, they were also conversing and debating about all the recent events. During this time, "Jesus himself drew near and walked with them, but their eyes were prevented from recognizing him."[248] As the men walked with the stranger, Jesus' identity was mysteriously veiled as it was when He encountered Mary Magdalene.

In the Gospel of John, we are told that "on the first day of the week, Mary of Magdala came to the tomb early in the morning, while it was still dark, and saw the stone removed from the tomb. So she ran and went to Simon Peter and to the other disciple whom Jesus loved, and told them."[249] Simon Peter and the other disciple, believed to be John, ran to the tomb. They entered the tomb and found only the burial cloths. As they exited the tomb, they saw Mary Magdalene sobbing with grief. They walked past her in deep thought. Mary, however, stayed near the tomb. The Gospel of John tells us that "as she wept, she bent over into the tomb and saw two angels in white sitting there, one at the head and one at the feet where the body of Jesus had been."[250] One of the angels spoke to Mary and asked, "Woman, why are you weeping?" She then replied, "They have taken my Lord, and I don't know where they laid him.'"[251] Perhaps she heard a noise that caused her to turn. When she turned, she saw Jesus there, but His identity was mysteriously veiled. She did not recognize Him. Jesus then asked the same question the angels asked earlier. "Woman, why are you weeping?" He then asked, "Whom are you looking for?"[252] The Gospel of John tells us that "she thought it was the gardener and said to him, 'Sir, if you carried him away, tell me where you laid him, and I will take him.'"[253] It was not until Jesus spoke Mary's name that she recognized Jesus and responded with joy by calling Him "*Rabbouni*, which means Teacher."[254]

On the surface of these findings, it seems that the Gospel of Luke and the Gospel of John have conflicting stories regarding what occurred at Jesus' tomb. How many women visited the tomb? When did the women visit the tomb? What did the risen Jesus say to the women? Did Peter and John go to the tomb, or did Peter go alone?

An article by Dave Armstrong stated that it seems to be a "favorite pastime of extreme biblical skeptics to peruse the Gospel accounts of the resurrection of Jesus and events surrounding it, in order to 'identify' and challenge Christians with various alleged 'contradictions.'" He further stated that none of the alleged contradictions are "adequately substantiated, once the claims were properly scrutinized." "Almost all of them," he stated, "failed even elementary tests of standard logic." An example of Armstrong's explanation focused on how many women visited the tomb. "An actual logical contradiction requires exclusionary clauses such as '*only x, y, z* were there and *no one else*' or '*only three people witnessed incident a.*' None of the Gospel texts do that here; hence, no demonstrable contradiction exists." Armstrong further stated that "some atheists will nonetheless go on to argue that it is still a 'contradiction' in *some* sense because, after all, the texts don't all *say exactly the same thing*." "But that's not how logic works," he explained, "and it is absurd and unrealistic to demand that four separate accounts written by as many people must report what was seen in *identical fashion*."[255]

In a similar way, Dr. Tim Chaffey addressed the possible conflict of when the women went to the tomb as well as how many went. "The Gospels," according to Chaffey, "refer to different times and name different women who arrived at the tomb." Chaffey pointed out that Matthew, in the Gospel of Matthew, stated that "Mary Magdalene and the other Mary" came to the tomb as it "began to dawn." In the Gospel of Mark, the writer "adds Salome to the group and claims that they came 'very early in the morning.'" Luke, in his Gospel, "agrees that it was 'very early in the morning' and names 'Mary Magdalene, Joanna, Mary the mother of James, and the other women' as those who came to the tomb." John, however, in his Gospel, "wrote that 'Mary Magdalene went to the tomb early, while it was still dark.'"[256]

Regarding the timing of the women's trip, Chaffey stated that "the sticky point is John's claim that they went to the tomb 'while it was still dark.'" He then asked, "Was it very early in the morning at dawn, or was it still dark?" Chaffey concluded that "John may have described when the women initially left for the tomb, while the other gospels described when the women arrived." Regarding the differences in the number of women, Chaffey stated that "at least five women went to the tomb since Luke names three of them and then says, 'other women' went too." He further noted that "Matthew does not say that *only* two women were there. Mark does not say *only* three women were there. They simply focus on the women they name. Although John named only Mary Magdalene, he was clearly aware that she was not alone." Chaffey further noted that Mary Magdalene, reporting to Peter and John, said, "They have taken away the Lord out of the tomb, and *we* do not know where they have laid Him." After close analysis, Chaffey concluded that "when we put all the pieces together, the wonder of the Resurrection shines out in even greater glory."[257]

The Resurrection had occurred. The tomb was empty. Mary Magdalene met Jesus in the garden but did not recognize Him until He spoke her name. In a similar way, the identity of Jesus was veiled for the two men walking to their homes in Emmaus. They were conversing with this stranger, who seemed to know more than he initially revealed. These men listened intently as this stranger spoke to them about the prophets, beginning with Moses. There was understanding in his words that all that had occurred was a fulfillment of Scripture. As the men moved closer to their village, the stranger gave "the impression that he was going on further."[258] They did not want Him to leave. This stranger was providing the explanation they longed for. They felt a connection to this man. However, they did not understand why that was so. He was a stranger, and they did not recognize Him. Nevertheless, they invited Him to stay with them. The stranger agreed and entered their home. After settling in from the long journey, they prepared a meal and reclined at the table. As they prepared to eat, the stranger took "bread, said the blessing, broke it, and gave it to them." At that moment, "their eyes were opened, and they recognized him." They gasped with their eyes and mouths wide open. It was Jesus, and their hearts were flooded with love and joy beyond measure. Before they could do or say anything, "he vanished from their sight."[259] However, in their hands, they had the bread that Jesus prayed over. Suddenly, they remembered His words, *"This is my body"* and acknowledged the prayer Jesus prayed in their presence. Jesus left them in one form but remained with them in the bread of the Eucharist. They also remembered the manna provided to their ancestors and how it provided nourishment for their journey. These men recognized that they must return to Jerusalem. They accepted the nourishment of Jesus' body to sustain them on this journey. Without hesitation, they ate the bread with the same reverence as the Passover meal. They gathered their belongings and again set out for Jerusalem. There was joy and excitement in their steps as they made their way back to the city of hope. As they entered Jerusalem, "they found gathered together the eleven and those with them who were saying, 'the Lord has truly been raised and has appeared to Simon!'"[260] They, too, had a story to tell. Jesus appeared to them as well and made Himself "known to them in the breaking of the bread."[261]

The *Catechism of the Catholic Church* teaches that God is "beyond space and time."[262] An article by Stephen M. Barr stated that "had God not chosen to create space and time, there would be no such things as space and time; so spatial and temporal categories cannot possibly apply to God's own nature." "God is 'eternal,'" Barr stated, "not in the sense of unlimited duration, but in the sense of timeless existence."[263] Because Jesus is God, the principles of God's existence apply to Him as well. Jesus appeared to Simon Peter and, at the same time, was walking with the men on the Road to Emmaus. St. Thomas Aquinas stated that "God lives in the *nunc stans*, 'the now that stands still.'"[264] There were no limitations to what God could do. He is as present to each of us today as He was to Simon Peter and the men on the road to Emmaus.

Reflection

As I consider the challenge of Saint Ignatius of Loyola to place myself in the scene, I decide to look beyond the story to consider the perspective of Mary Magdalene as she listens to the men share their experiences.

I am so happy to know that Jesus is back with us. Seeing Him at the tomb was remarkable beyond words. Yet, I manage to share all that I witnessed with the apostles and the other disciples. Now, Peter has also seen Jesus, and he, too, is sharing his experience. We do not know where Jesus is at this present time, but there is immense joy and happiness among all of us. After Peter's testimony, the women begin planning the next meal. The men, led by Peter, move to a separate part of the room. Suddenly, there is a knock at the door. Cleopas and his friend, Philip, enter. With great joy, Cleopas asks, "Where is Peter?" Peter immediately stands and looks toward the men. Cleopas walks toward Peter and warmly embraces him. Gazing intently into Peter's eyes, Cleopas says, "We've seen Him. We've seen Jesus." Peter smiles and says, "I know. I've seen Him, too."

All activity in the room stops as we gather around these two men. I bring a pitcher with two cups and serve them fresh water from our well. We then listen to all that they say. Cleopas tells the story of how they walked seven miles from Jerusalem to their village in Emmaus with a man that they did not recognize. Philip, the friend traveling with Cleopas, shakes his head and says, "I can't believe I did not recognize him." Cleopas then continues, "He spoke so eloquently about the prophets and Moses and that the crucifixion was a fulfillment of scripture." Cleopas also begins shaking his head and says, "I didn't recognize him either." With that, I speak up and say, "Neither did I." I then share with them my experience with Jesus at the tomb and how I thought He was a gardener until he spoke my name. Cleopas' eyes widen as he says, "That happened with us, too. But for us, we recognized Him in the breaking of the bread. And then, He vanished." With those words, Cleopas raises his hands and eyes toward heaven. He then continues, "In our hands was the bread he blessed. I immediately remember His words from the Passover meal – *this is my body*. I also clearly remember the story of the manna provided to our ancestors for the journey and how Jesus referred to Himself as the bread from heaven. It became obvious to both of us that Jesus is still present to us, but this time in the bread. We ate the bread before making the journey back to all of you. That bread has sustained us, and I truly believe that it always will." I am in awe at all that has occurred and wonder what will happen next.

++++++++++

Prayerfully consider the journey taken by Cleopas and his friend. Have you ever spent so much time thinking about something and getting nowhere in understanding the issue? Spend time sharing your thoughts with Our Lord and acknowledging His presence in the Eucharist.

PRAYER NOTES

PRAYER NOTES

Chapter 12

The Marriage Supper of the Lamb

Chapter 12

The Marriage Supper of the Lamb

The Book of Revelation has always been a challenge to read. However, the introduction to the Book of Revelation provided by Father Stephen Grunow in the *Word on Fire Bible* sheds light on its true meaning. Father Grunow stated that "the meaning of the book of Revelation is disclosed only when the text is understood as telling us about Christ." This book, Father Grunow stated, "is a revelation about Him [Christ]." The strangeness of the writings found in the Book of Revelation were, as noted by Father Grunow, "a result of our being drawn out of the narrowness of our limited interpretation of God and the world and into God's vantage point." In addition, Father Grunow pointed out that "our understanding of reality is a projection of what we want reality to be, and the result is an ego-drama." However, the true reality, as noted by Father Grunow, "is a theo-drama, where God is at the center rather than ourselves."[265]

Father Grunow explained that the Book of Revelation was "written for the Church." He also stated that the book is a "text of persecution." By this, he meant that "the genre that is employed is expressive of a crisis that is deeply personal." He continued by stating that "even if the world is not literally ending, it seems that way to the persecuted."[266]

The Book of Revelation is divided into seven parts. The fifth part is entitled *The Punishment of Babylon and the Destruction of Pagan Nations.*[267] It is in this section that the Scriptures are found concerning the last station of the Eucharist, entitled – *The Marriage Supper of the Lamb.*

"Let us rejoice and exult and give him the glory, for the marriage of the Lamb has come, and his bride has made herself ready; to her it has been granted to be clothed with fine linen, bright and pure" – for the fine linen is the righteous deeds of the saints.

And the angel said to me, "Write this: Blessed are those who are invited to the marriage supper of the Lamb." And he said to me, "These are true words of God." **Rev 19:7-9 – The Word on Fire Bible**

The Bible, according to Bishop Barron, "is filled with the imagery of marriage." Adam and Eve, he noted, were "the first married couple." In addition, Bishop Barron pointed out that the Book of Revelation speaks of the wedding banquet of the Lamb where "Christ is the Bridegroom, and his Bride the Church."

Bishop Barron further stated that "in the Incarnation, heaven and earth are joined – divinity and humanity come together in a *sacrum connubium*, a holy marriage.[268] However, the marriage supper of the Lamb is not only Christ's union with the Church. "Christ is also the Bridegroom of our souls," as noted in an article by Dr. Edward Sri. "Every time we receive Jesus in Holy Communion," Sri stated, "we are invited into the marriage supper of the Lamb, the heavenly banquet, the mystical wedding feast of the Lamb mentioned in the book of Revelation." In the Mass, after the consecration, the priest says, *Blessed are those who are called to the supper of the Lamb.* "The most profound image that portrays God's closeness," according to Sri, "is that of marriage." The beautiful prayer said by the priest at every Mass, Sri stated, "awakens us to the reality that Holy Communion is profoundly marital because it is Jesus Himself coming down to dwell within us and unite Himself to us."[269]

An article by Scott Hahn stated that "it is an angel" in the Book of Revelation that says, *Blessed are those who have been called to the wedding feast of the Lamb.* "We're not just happy when we attend the liturgy," said Hahn. "We are blessed." He further stated that "we go to heaven when we go to Mass." The word *blessed*, according to Hahn, "connects us with the Scriptures, Old Testament and New, in a profound way." "To be blessed," according to Hahn, "is the divinely ordained consequence of fidelity to the covenant." Hahn further noted that "the supper of the Lamb is the Passover of the New Covenant." Hahn indicated that the Old Covenant Passover "was not just a meal, but a sacrifice – a sacrifice that brought about reconciliation, atonement, and communion." Hahn pointed to the fact that "in the Eucharist, we celebrate Jesus' permanent, fruitful, ecstatic communion with the Church" and noted further that "what begins now will continue in heaven where 'we shall see him as he is.'"[270]

Mark Shea, in an article on this station, stated that "realty, like the Mass, is consummated with the Marriage Supper of the Lamb." He further noted that Jesus "describes the Kingdom of Heaven as a wedding feast." Shea pointed out that the apostles "take up the thread of thought by seeing every marriage between baptized individuals as a participation in this mystical marriage between Christ the Bridegroom and his Bride the Church."[271] Shea also pointed to the words of Saint Paul in the Letter to the Ephesians.

> *As the church is subordinate to Christ, so wives should be subordinate to their husbands in everything. Husbands, love your wives, even as Christ loved the church and handed himself over for her to sanctify her, cleansing her by the bath of water with the word, that he might present to*

himself the church in splendor, without spot or wrinkle or any such thing, that she might be holy and without blemish. So also husbands should love their wives as their own bodies. He who loves his wife loves himself. For no one hates his own flesh but rather nourishes and cherishes it, even as Christ does the church, because we are members of his body...This is a great mystery, but I speak in reference to Christ and the church. **Ephesians 5:24-32**

The "early Fathers of the Church," as noted by Shea, considered John's language regarding the Marriage Supper of the Lamb not only as a reference "to the cosmic union of the Bridegroom and Bride at the end of time but also as a reference to the Eucharist." "The Eucharist," Shea noted, "is a participation in and an anticipation of the mystical Marriage Feast of the Lamb and the Consummation of All Things."[272]

Previously noted in this writing, in the Seventh Station of the Eucharist, we learned of the three stages of the marriage ceremony of biblical times. The second stage, which took place prior to the wedding feast, was the sexual consummation of marriage. When we participate in the Eucharist, we consume Jesus. We become one with Him when we receive Him – Body, Blood, Soul, and Divinity in the Eucharist. "Our marriage to the Lamb of God," as noted in an article by Father Pedro A. Moreno, "is renewed and consummated again and again at every Mass." Father Moreno further stated that "as we approach the altar, the minister shows us our loving groom in all his glory and says, 'Body of Christ.' We who are hungry for love and mercy, hungry for God, hungry for the word, hungry for Christ say, 'Amen.'" "The Church, the bride, all of the baptized present and living in a state of sanctifying grace," according to Father Moreno, "are once again reunited with our loving and life-giving groom Jesus Christ, really and truly alive and present under the appearances of bread and wine." "Our senses are deceived," Father Moreno said, "but our hearts see a reality that transcends the eyes."[273] The *Catechism of the Catholic Church* stated that "the Church knows that the Lord comes even now in his Eucharist and that he is there in our midst. However, his presence is veiled. Therefore, we celebrate the Eucharist 'awaiting the blessed hope and the coming of our Savior, Jesus Christ.'"[274]

Reflection

As I considered the reflection for this station, I thought for a long time about where to place myself in this Scripture. We find angels loving and praising God. Jesus is also front and center as the ultimate bridegroom. The bride noted in the Scripture is the Church.

I spend a lot of time and in different ways building my relationship with Jesus and getting to know Him better. I attend Mass regularly and receive Him in the Eucharist. I attend Bible studies and retreats to increase my knowledge and love for Him. However, I also realize from this study that I must consider that my relationship with Jesus is not only personal. I am but one member of the entire Body of Christ. There are many other members. Who are these members? Do they think like me? Would I consider them a friend? What happens if I do not like those other members who are joined with me?

I can hear all the beautiful voices of the angels praising God. The sound is so beautiful, making it difficult to find words to describe it. The voices of the Pope's personal choir, known as the Sistine Chapel Choir, come close to what I am hearing. But, in so many ways, it is so much better. Somehow, I did not think that was possible. There are people gathering all around me. I know that the Body of Christ is forming around me. We are the Church. We are the bride of Christ. I recognize some of these people. However, most of them are strangers.

Suddenly, I see in the distance a woman I met briefly at a non-related church event. It was not a good encounter. She was rude and lashed out at me when I spoke to her. I do not remember the details of the encounter. But I certainly remember her face and the way she made me feel that day. I also remember learning the importance of forgiveness through that encounter. On that day when the incident occurred, I remember walking away from her, distraught and deeply hurt. The word *forgiveness* sprung up within me. I immediately prayed, "Lord, I forgive her." That evening, however, I tossed and turned as the incident replayed repeatedly in my mind. I remember getting out of bed and sitting quietly in my favorite chair with my Bible in hand. I slowly prayed the Our Father. I then remembered a book I recently read on the importance of prayer. In that book, I learned about forgiveness in a way I had not considered before.

The book is still resting on my coffee table. I open the book and re-read the chapter on forgiveness.

"Forgiveness," I read, "doesn't mean condoning, minimizing, or excusing a hurt done to us. It doesn't mean surrendering a right to justice when, for example, someone has stolen from us."[275] I pause for a few minutes and think about these words as they relate to the encounter I experienced earlier. I then continue reading, "Forgiveness is a decision to let go of a hurt done to us. It is the gift we give ourselves so we do not allow the hurt to control our emotions." The author then adds a quote from Jean Maalouf. "Forgiveness is the powerful assertion that bad things will not ruin your today even though they may have spoiled your past." The final sentence on this page states that "we know that forgiveness is occurring when the distance between our offender and us is peaceful and not hostile." I do not feel hostility toward this woman; however, I also do not feel peace. Deep within me, I could hear myself with indignation say, *How dare she speak to me in that way?*

As I continue to flip through the chapter on forgiveness, I come to the section that provides three prayer suggestions. The third suggestion states that "it is always helpful to keep in mind that people hurt us or fail us not because they are evil monsters, but because they, like us, are imperfect, wounded, and sinful people." The author reminds me that "just as we often need God's mercy and the mercy of others, we need to be ready, with God's grace, to share his mercy with others." This section of the book then displays a beautiful prayer, which I pray reverently and with an open heart.

> *Lord, you created (this woman) wonderfully just as you created me. You love this person just as you love me – with all my faults and weaknesses. You know I don't love this person very much at this time, but you do. Share with me your love for her. Also, God, I ask you to bless this scoundrel. Sometimes I, too, am a scoundrel and in need of your blessing.*

After saying this prayer, I close my eyes and again slowly repeat the Our Father. This time, however, the words, *forgive us our trespasses as we forgive those who trespass against us*, bring a clearer understanding. Forgiveness is truly a gift we give ourselves. It is a grace that we accept from the Father. We do not deserve forgiveness, yet He freely gives it to each of us. This grace, like all graces, must be shared. And so, we must never judge others as to whether they deserve forgiveness. Forgiveness should be freely given as it has been given to each of us by Our Father. Sometimes, we spend a lot of time learning ways to keep our physical bodies healthy. One way that we can ensure a healthy spirit is to allow the grace of forgiveness to flow to us from God and through us to others.

I never saw that woman again until this moment in heaven as we gather as the Body of Christ, the Church, and the beautiful Bride of Christ. Our prayers are very important, and we do not know the impact of the simplest prayers. I wonder for a moment what the outcome might have been if I had withheld forgiveness. Would I see that woman in heaven as I see her now? Would I even be here?

I close my eyes and breathe in deeply, thanking God for all that He has taught me. I then hear the voice of an angel who clearly announces, *Blessed are those who have been called to the wedding feast of the Lamb.* As I hear the word *blessed* from the angelic voice, I immediately realize its deeper meaning. As humans, we struggle with the ego and the tendency toward sin. We consider our performance in the ego-drama to be worthy of great reward. However, the cross that Jesus asks us to carry is the shift we must make from the ego-drama to the theo-drama where He, rather than us, is at the center of our lives. All of us present, including my new friend, have experienced the pain of the cross and have embraced the goodness of God and the immense love He has for His Church. Because of this, we are all truly blessed.

++++++++++

Prayerfully consider your membership in the Body of Christ. We all have a role to play. Consider the talents and gifts you share with others. Spend time with Our Lord talking about the difficulty of forgiveness. Perhaps you are struggling with accepting forgiveness from God or sharing forgiveness for a past hurt. God is always with us and ready to listen. Share with him your hurts and then spend time in His presence listening. He always has something to say to us.

PRAYER NOTES

PRAYER NOTES

Conclusion

Conclusion

The Stations of the Eucharist provide a clear understanding of the truths of the Eucharist. Jesus is truly present to us in this Blessed Sacrament. Do we dare to courageously defend Jesus in the Eucharist? Many saints have done just that. Every saint of the Catholic Church has been deeply devoted to the Blessed Sacrament.

"From the dawn of Christian history," as noted in an article by Father John A. Hardon, S.J., "faith in the Holy Eucharist as the living Christ has been continuous." Father Hardon further stated that because of the truths of the Eucharist, "we have writers like Saint Ignatius of Antioch, Saint Justin the martyr, Saint Irenaeus, Saint Cyprian, and many others, all attesting to the presence of the living Christ in the Holy Eucharist through the words of consecration at Mass."[276]

Corpus Christi Sunday, also known as the Solemnity of the Most Holy Body and Blood of Christ, "was originally proposed as a feast day by Saint Thomas Aquinas." This special feast day honors the Eucharist, "reminding all to recognize that it is the True Presence – the Body and Blood, Soul and Divinity of Christ." Saint Thomas Aquinas stated that "the Eucharist is the sacrament of love: it signifies love, it produces love." "The Eucharist," as noted by Saint Thomas Aquinas, "is the consummation of the whole spiritual life."[277]

Saint Francis de Sales was a scholar, writer, pastor, diplomat, bishop, and Doctor of the Church who lived more than 400 years ago. His book, *The Catholic Controversy, A Defense of the Faith*, stated that his preaching and writings were "so clear and thorough that at the end of four years, nearly the entire population of 72,000 had returned to the Catholic faith."[278] Regarding the Eucharist, Saint Francis de Sales stated that "when the bee has gathered the dew of heaven and the earth's sweetest nectar from the flowers, it turns it into honey, then hastens to its hive. In the same way, the priest, having taken from the altar the Son of God (who is as the dew from heaven, and true son of Mary, flower of our humanity), gives him to you as delicious food."[279]

Saint Cyril of Jerusalem was a theologian of the early Church. He succeeded Maximus as Bishop of Jerusalem in the year 350 A.D. and was declared a Doctor of the Church in 1822. Regarding the Eucharist, Saint Cyril emphatically stated, "Since Christ Himself has said, 'This is My Body,' who shall dare to doubt it is His Body?"[280]

Even in our modern time, the Catholic Church has recognized a young man, soon to be canonized as a saint, who had a great love for Jesus in the Eucharist. Blessed Carlo Acutis was born in 1991. An article by Francesca Pollio Fenton and Courtney Mares stated that "from a young age, Carlo had a special love for God...After he made his first Communion, he went to Mass as often as possible at the parish across from his elementary school." Fenton and Mares noted that "Carlo's love for the Eucharist also inspired a deep conversion for his mother," who admitted that she only "went to Mass for her first Communion, her confirmation, and her wedding." Fenton and Mares shared that Carlo "wasn't afraid to defend Church teaching, even in situations when his classmates disagreed with him." During a classroom discussion about abortion, Fenton and Mares stated that several of his classmates remember Carlo giving a "passionate defense for the protection of life from the moment of conception." They further noted that Carlo "was known for standing up for kids at school who got bullied, especially kids with disabilities."[281]

As a young man, Carlo was fascinated with computer coding. Fenton and Mares stated in their article that "Carlo taught himself some of the basic coding languages...and used his computer skills and internet savvy to help his family put together an exhibition on Eucharistic miracles."[282]

This exhibition has been displayed at "thousands of parishes on five continents." I had the opportunity to see this exhibition at a local parish near my home. The research and presentation in the exhibits were quite extensive and included over 20 countries. Carlo's spiritual director, as noted by Fenton and Mares, "attested that Carlo was personally convinced that the scientific evidence from Eucharistic miracles would help people to realize that Jesus is really present in the Eucharist and come back to Mass."[283] The scientific proof provided in the exhibit was amazing, especially as it related to the most recent miracles.

For example, there were three Eucharistic miracles that occurred in 1992, 1994, and again in 1996 in Buenos Aires, Argentina. Pope Francis was the archbishop of Buenos Aires at the time. The testament of the miracle is as follows: "In 1992, after the Mass of Friday, May 1, while preparing the Eucharistic reserve, a Eucharistic minister found some pieces of consecrated Host on the corporal. Following what the Church prescribes to do in these situations, the priest had (the pieces) put in a vessel of water, which was placed in the Tabernacle to wait for them to dissolve. In the following days, several priests went to check it, and they realized that nothing had changed. Seven days later, on Friday, May 8, they opened the tabernacle and saw that the Host fragments had become a reddish color that looked like blood. The following Sunday, May 10, during the two evening Masses, several small drops of blood were noticed on the patens with which the priests distributed Communion."

"On Sunday, July 24, 1994, during the children's Mass, while the Eucharistic minister took the pix from the tabernacle, he saw a drop of blood running along its side."

"On August 15, 1996, during the Mass of the Assumption of the Most Holy Virgin, a consecrated Host, which fell to the ground during the distribution of Communion, had to be placed again in a vessel of water so it would dissolve. A few days later, on August 26, a Eucharistic minister opened the Tabernacle and saw that Host had transformed into Blood."

Archbishop Bergoglio, known today as Pope Francis, called Professor Ricardo Castanon Gomez to analyze the miracle that occurred on August 15, 1996. Professor Gomez began his investigation by interviewing the priests involved as well as a lady parishioner who was a chemist. The lady chemist, after analysis of the bleeding Host, discovered that it was human blood. She also noted that "the blood had active white blood cells, which normally are around only in the presence of infection." Several other physicians were called in to examine the Hosts, including Doctor Frederick Zugibe, who is a world-renowned expert not only in forensic pathology but also in cardiology. Doctor Zugibe spent most of his career as the chief medical examiner of Rockland County, New York. On his retirement in 2003, he estimated his office had completed 10,000 autopsies during his tenure. Following his examination of the Host, Doctor Zugibe stated, "I am an expert on the heart. The heart is my business. This is flesh. This flesh is heart muscle tissue, myocardium, from the left ventricle wall not far from a valvular area. It is the muscle that gives the heart its beat and the body its life. The heart muscle is inflamed. It has lost its striations and is infiltrated with white blood cells. White blood cells are not normally found in heart tissue. These cells are produced by the body, and they escape from blood and infiltrate the tissue to address trauma or injury."[284]

Another Eucharistic miracle, verified on May 5, 2011, took place in India in 2001. The parish priest of St. Mary's Church in Chirattakonam, India, provided the testimony for this event. "At 8:49 a.m., I exposed the Most Holy Sacrament in the monstrance for public adoration. After a few moments, I saw what appeared to be three dots in the Holy Eucharist. I then stopped praying and began to look at the monstrance, also inviting the faithful to admire the three dots. I then asked the faithful to remain in prayer and reposed the monstrance in the Tabernacle... On Saturday morning, the 5th of May 2001, I opened the church for the usual liturgical celebrations. I vested for Mass and went to open the tabernacle to see what had happened to the Eucharist in the monstrance. I immediately noted in the Host a figure to the likeness of a human face. I was deeply moved and asked the faithful to kneel and begin praying. I thought I alone could see the face, so I asked the altar server what he noticed in the monstrance. He answered, 'I see the figure of a man.'"[285] Eventually, the image became clearer and was of a man like that of Christ crowned with thorns. In response to this miracle, the Archbishop of Trivandrum wrote, "...For us believers, what we have seen is something that we have always believed..." The monstrance containing this miraculous Host is to this day kept in St. Mary's Church in Chirattakonam, India.[286]

The most recent Eucharistic miracle noted in the Miracles List on Blessed Carlo Acutis' website occurred in Sokolka, Poland, in 2008. An article by Father Robert J. Spitzer, S.J. provided a summary of what took place in 2008 at the church of Saint Anthony.[287]

"That morning during Mass, a priest accidentally dropped a host while distributing Communion. The Host was then put in a small container of water. The pastor, Father Stanislaw Gniedziejko, asked the sacristan, Sister Julia Dubowska of the Congregation of the Eucharistic Sisters, to place the container in a safe in the sacristy. After a week, Sister Julia checked on the Host. When she opened the safe, she smelled something like unleavened bread, and the Host had a red blood stain on it."

"Immediately, Sister Julia and Father Gniedziejko told the archbishop of Bialystok...about the Host. The bishop had the stained Host taken out of the container and placed on a corporal, where it stayed in the tabernacle for three years. During this time, the stained fragment of the Host dried out (appearing more like a blood stain or clot), and several studies were commissioned on the Host. The studies found that the altered fragment of the Host is identical to the myocardial (heart) tissue of a person who is nearing death. Additionally, the structure of the muscle fibers and that of the bread are interwoven in a way impossible to produce by human means."

A more recent Eucharistic miracle noted in Father Spitzer's article took place on Christmas Day 2013 at the Church of Saint Hyacinth in Legnica, Poland. On that day in 2013, "a consecrated Host fell on the floor. The Host was put into a container with water so that it would dissolve. Instead, it formed red stains. In February 2014, the Host was examined by various research institutes, including the Department of Forensic Medicine in Szczecin." Their findings stated that "in the histopathological image, the fragments were found containing the fragmented parts of the cross-striated muscle. It is most similar to the heart muscle." Father Spitzer's article further stated that the findings of the 2013 miracle in Poland were like earlier findings of Eucharistic miracles in Italy in that "the research found that the tissue had alterations that would appear during great distress."

"The bleeding Host of Poland," as noted by Father Spitzer, "was approved for veneration in April 2016 by Bishop Zbigniew Kiernikowski of Legnica, who said that it 'has the hallmarks of a Eucharistic miracle.'"

Although it is by faith that we accept the truth of the Eucharistic presence of Our Lord and Savior, Jesus Christ, sometimes God provides the physical proof we need to accept all that He is doing for us. Faith is a process. We learn more every day. It is up to us to ask the questions and dig for the answers. If it has been a while since you've been to Mass, I encourage you to attend the next Catholic Mass scheduled in your area. God's door is always open. It is up to us to choose Him. If you are not Catholic, consider witnessing the beauty of the Mass and the presence of Our Lord Jesus in the Tabernacle of every Catholic church. The Order of Christian Initiation of Adults (OCIA) is available for the formation of adults, whether you are new to the Catholic faith or have been away for a long time.

Our God is a God of details. He thinks of everything when it comes to our well-being. To assist us in the journey of life, He makes Himself available to us in the Eucharist. The Eucharist is love as God is love. Be encouraged, and do not fear. The Lord is present in the

Eucharist and waits for you to accept Him in this special way.

++++++++++

National Eucharistic Revival Prayer[288]

Lord Jesus Christ, you give us your flesh and blood for the life of the world, and you desire that all people come to the Supper of the Sacrifice of the Lamb. Renew in your Church the truth, beauty, and goodness contained in the Most Blessed Eucharist.

Jesus living in the Eucharist, come and live in me.

Jesus healing in the Eucharist, come and heal me.

Jesus sacrificing yourself in the Eucharist, come and suffer in me.

Jesus rising in the Eucharist, come and rise to new life in me.

Jesus loving in the Eucharist, come and love in me.

Lord Jesus Christ, through the paschal mystery of your death and resurrection made present in every Holy Mass, pour out your healing love on your Church and on our world. Grant that as we lift you up during this time of Eucharistic Revival, your Holy Spirit may draw all people to join us at this Banquet of Life. You live and reign with the Father and the Holy Spirit, God forever and ever.

Amen!

Acknowledgments

Writing is a solo adventure. God provides the ideas that materialize on paper as a manuscript. Publishing a manuscript, however, is a group adventure that involves the talents of many key people. I am grateful for my friend, Jan Carnahan, who provided theological insight for the initial review of this book. I am also grateful to Very Reverend Joseph L. Waters, Censor Librorum, at the Diocese of Saint Petersburg, Florida. Father Waters' review resulted in the *Nihil Obstat* award for this book.

My friend, Nermine Khouzam Rubin challenged me to ask our bishop to write the Foreword for this book. I am grateful for the love and support of my bishop, Most Reverend Gregory Parkes, who did not hesitate in writing the Foreword. It is truly a blessing to not only have the encouragement and support of friends but also to have the love and support of my bishop as I share with all of you the writings that God has put on my heart.

Once again, I am also grateful for the amazing editing done by Ellen Gable Hrkach and Innate Productions. The editing process continued with the professional support of Nick Lauer and Mary Ann Skin.

I am truly grateful for the leading of the Holy Spirit in all that I write. Getting the book into the hands of God's people requires a professionally designed book cover. This was achieved by the expertise of James Hrkach at Full Quiver Publishing-Innate Productions.

As a new member of the Associates of the Sisters of Notre Dame, I am reminded daily of God's goodness. His love and kindness are found in all that we encounter. We must take the time to acknowledge Him in all things. I thank God daily for my husband, John, and my son, Danny, who I know pray for me from heaven above. I am also very grateful for the love and support from all my family and friends as I move forward in doing all that God asks of me.

About the Author

Denise Mercado is an award-winning author, blogger, solo traveler, widow, mother, and grandmother. Denise was born and raised in Brooklyn, New York and Plainview, Long Island. As a military spouse, she lived in many cities throughout the USA and abroad.

Denise has a Bachelor of Science from Campbell University, is an active member of her parish in Palm Harbor, Florida, and an Associate with the Sisters of Notre Dame. Denise received book awards from the Catholic Media Association, Independent Author Network, and Readers' Favorite. The Diocese of Saint Petersburg awarded the **Nihil Obstat** in 2023 for her book – *The Way of Light: The Story Behind the Stations of the Resurrection.* The **Nihil Obstat** was also awarded in 2024 for her latest book – *The Stations of the Eucharist: from Melchizedek to the Book of Revelation.*

Denise is a solo traveler. She explores the beauty and history of the Catholic Church by visiting cathedrals, basilicas, monasteries, and shrines and writing about her findings in her **Catholic Travel Blog.** For more information about Denise's books, blogs, and travel plans, visit her website at www.denisemercado.com.

CONNECT WTH DENISE

Thank you so much for taking the time to read this book. I enjoy sharing with you all that God has shown me as I study and build my relationship with Him.

If you have any questions, feel free to contact me at denise@denisemercado.com.

You can also connect with me on Facebook at https://www.facebook.com/denisemercadoauthor/

If you enjoyed this book, then I know you will enjoy my other books. Sign up at the website below to receive updates on new book releases and other book recommendations that will enhance your faith journey.

Updates on my Catholic Travel Blog will also be included when you sign up at the website below.

www.denisemercado.com

Other Books by Denise Mercado

Mary's Life Journey & Her Amazing Yes! – Award Winner – 2023 Catholic Media Association Book Awards; 2023 Independent Author Network; 2024 Readers' Favorite

My Prayer Journey through the Mysteries of ALL the Rosaries!

The Way of Light: The Story Behind the Stations of the Resurrection – *Awarded the Nihil Obstat in 2023 from the Diocese of Saint Petersburg, Florida*

Divine Threads: My Journey of Faith and Blessings – *co-authored with Father Pedro Camilo Simoes, SAC*

The Stations of the Eucharist: from Melchizedek to the Book of Revelation – *Awarded the Nihil Obstat in 2024 from the Diocese of Saint Petersburg, Florida*

They Created Us

For more information about Denise's books, visit her website at
  https://www.denisemercado.com/books-by-denise

ENDNOTES

[1] Father William Saunders, "How Did the Stations of the Cross Begin?" *Catholic Education Resource Center*, Accessed 29 November 2023, https://www.catholiceducation.org/en/culture/catholic-contributions/how-did-the-stations-of-the-cross-begin.html

[2] Philip Kosloski, Have you ever prayed the Stations of the Eucharist?, Aleteia, 1 June 2018, https://aleteia.org/2018/06/01/have-you-ever-prayed-the-stations-of-the-eucharist/, (accessed 17 November 2023)

[3] Shrine of the Blessed Sacrament, Hanceville, Alabama, https://www.olamshrine.com/visit/things-to-do

[4] Genesis 13:9 NAB

[5] Genesis 13:10 NAB

[6] Genesis 13:13 NAB

[7] Genesis 13:15 NAB

[8] Genesis 13:18 NAB

[9] Genesis 14:9 NAB

[10] Genesis 14: 10-17 NAB

[11] Genesis 14:19-20 NAB

[12] Genesis 18:1 NAB

[13] Moses Y. Lee, Who is Melchizedek?, 17 June 2020, *The Gospel Coalition*, Bible and Theology, https://www.thegospelcoalition.org/article/jesus-melchizedek/, (accessed 17 March 2024)

[14] Psalm 110:1 NAB

[15] Pope shows how Psalm 110 foresaw coming of Jesus, *Catholic News Agency*, Vatican City, 16 November 2011, https://www.catholicnewsagency.com/news/23777/pope-shows-how-psalm-110-foresaw-coming-of-jesus#:~:text=Pope%20Benedict%20summed%20up%20Psalm,'%E2%80%9D, (accessed 17 March 2024)

[16] St Robert Bellarmine's commentary on Psalm 110, The Divine Lamp, 21 December 2016, https://thedivinelamp.wordpress.com/2016/12/21/st-robert-bellarmines-commentary-on-psalm-110/, (accessed 17 March 2024)

[17] Matthew 21:41-45 NAB

[18] St Robert Bellarmine's commentary on Psalm 110, The Divine Lamp, 21 December 2016,

https://thedivinelamp.wordpress.com/2016/12/21/st-robert-bellarmines-commentary-on-psalm-110/, (accessed 17 March 2024)

[19] Aaron, Oxford Bibliographies, 23 November 2021, https://www.oxfordbibliographies.com/display/document/obo-9780195393361/obo-9780195393361-0121.xml#:~:text=obo%2F9780195393361%2D0121-,Introduction,is%20seen%20as%20a%20priest., (accessed 17 March 2024)

[20] St Robert Bellarmine's commentary on Psalm 110, The Divine Lamp, 21 December 2016, https://thedivinelamp.wordpress.com/2016/12/21/st-robert-bellarmines-commentary-on-psalm-110/, (accessed 17 March 2024)

[21] St Robert Bellarmine's commentary on Psalm 110, The Divine Lamp, 21 December 2016, https://thedivinelamp.wordpress.com/2016/12/21/st-robert-bellarmines-commentary-on-psalm-110/, (accessed 17 March 2024)

[22] [22] Catholic Straight Answers, Who was Melchizedek?, https://catholicstraightanswers.com/who-was-melchizedek/#:~:text=The%20Catechism%20teaches%2C%20%E2%80%9CThe%20Christian,are%20sanctified%2C'%20that%20is%2C, (accessed 17 March 2024)

[23] Catechism of the Catholic Church, Second Edition, Section 58

[24] Catechism of the Catholic Church, Second Edition, Section 1333

[25] Catechism of the Catholic Church, Second Edition, Section 1544

[26] Institute of Catholic Culture, Who is Melchizedek?, Catholic Adult Education, https://instituteofcatholicculture.org/articles/who-is-melchizedek/, (accessed 3 February 2024)

[27] Father Charles Grondin, Was Melchizedek Jesus?, *Catholic Answers Q&A*, https://www.catholic.com/qa/was-melchizedek-jesus, (accessed 3 February 2024)

[28] Catholic Straight Answers, Who was Melchizedek?, https://catholicstraightanswers.com/who-was-melchizedek/#:~:text=The%20Catechism%20teaches%2C%20%E2%80%9CThe%20Christian,are%20sanctified%2C'%20that%20is%2C, (accessed 3 February 2024)

[29] Institute of Catholic Culture, Who is Melchizedek?, Catholic Adult Education, https://instituteofcatholicculture.org/articles/who-is-melchizedek/, (accessed 3 February 2024)

[30] Chapter VII: The Choice of the Masses and Its Parts, United States Conference of Catholic Bishops, https://www.usccb.org/prayer-and-worship/the-mass/general-instruction-of-the-roman-missal/girm-chapter-7#:~:text=a)%20Eucharistic%20Prayer%20I%2C%20or,pray)%20and%20also%20in%20the, (accessed 17 March 2024)

[31] Basic Texts for the Roman Catholic Eucharist, Eucharistic Prayers I-IV, https://catholic-resources.org/ChurchDocs/EP1-4.htm#:~:text=Look%20with%20favor%20on%20these,to%20your%20altar%20in%20heaven., (accessed 17 March 2024)

[32] Genesis 14:20(b) NAB

[33] JP Nunez, Melchizedek and the Mass, *Catholic Exchange*, 14 April 2023, https://catholicexchange.com/melchizedek-and-the-mass/, (accessed 20 March 2024)

[34] Scott Hahn, The Meal of Melchizedek, *EWTN*, https://www.ewtn.com/catholicism/teachings/meal-of-melchizedek-227, (accessed 20 March 2024)

[35] Exodus 32:1-29 NAB

[36] Scott Hahn, The Meal of Melchizedek, *EWTN*, https://www.ewtn.com/catholicism/teachings/meal-of-melchizedek-227, (accessed 20 March 2024)

[37] Catechism of the Catholic Church, Second Edition, Section 1324

[38] Wikipedia, The Ten Commandments (1956 film), https://en.wikipedia.org/wiki/The_Ten_Commandments_(1956_film), (accessed 22 March 2024)

[39] Exodus 5:1 – 13:16 (NAB)

[40] Exodus 11:1 (NAB)

[41] John 1:29 (NAB)

[42] Luke 1:41 (NAB)

[43] John 1:29 (NAB)

[44] Exodus 12:3 (NAB)

[45] Procure Definition & Meaning, Meriam-Webster, https://www.merriam-webster.com/dictionary/procure, (accessed 25 March 2024)

[46] Exodus 12:6 (NAB)

[47] Brant Pitre, Jesus and the Jewish Roots of the Eucharist, Published in the United States by Image, an imprint of the Crown Publishing Group, a division of Penguin Random House LLC, New York, 2011, 2016), page 52

[48] Exodus 12:7 (NAB)

[49] Exodus 24:8 (NAB)

[50] John 6:55 (NAB)
[51] Matthew 26:28 (NAB)
[52] John 19:34 (NAB)
[53] Chaplet of Divine Mercy, USCCB, Diary of Saint Faustina, Section 84, https://www.usccb.org/prayers/chaplet-divine-mercy, (accessed 25 March 2024)
[54] Matthew 5:17-18
[55] Catechism of the Catholic Church, Second Edition, Section 1340
[56] Exodus 11 & 12 (NAB)
[57] Exodus 12:4 (NAB)
[58] Wikipedia, Wilderness of Sin, https://en.wikipedia.org/wiki/Wilderness_of_Sin#:~:text=The%20Wilderness%20of%20Sin%20or,Hebrew%20name%20for%20this%20region., (accessed 10 April 2024)
[59] What is the Wilderness of Sin?, Got Questions.org, https://www.gotquestions.org/Wilderness-of-Sin.html, (accessed 10 April 2024)
[60] Exodus 16:1 (NAB)
[61] Exodus 16:3 (NAB)
[62] Manna, Catholic Encyclopedia, https://www.newadvent.org/cathen/09604a.htm#:~:text=(Greek%20man%2C%20manna%3B%20Latin,the%20appearance%20of%20hoar%20frost., (accessed 10 April 2024)
[63] Exodus 16:4 (NAB)
[64] Exodus 16:12 (NAB)
[65] What were the quail mentioned in the Bible?, Got Quesitons.org, https://www.gotquestions.org/quail-in-the-Bible.html, (accessed 11 April 2024)
[66] Professor Jonathan Jacobs, The Double Quail Narrative and Bekhor Shor's Innovative Reading, *The Torah.com*, https://www.thetorah.com/article/the-double-quail-narratives-and-bekhor-shors-innovative-reading, (accessed 11 April 2024)
[67] Exodus 16:13-14 (NAB)
[68] Exodus 16:15 (NAB)
[69] What was manna?, Got Questions.org, https://www.gotquestions.org/what-was-manna.html, (accessed 11 April 2024)
[70] Exodus 16:16 (NAB)
[71] Footnote for Exodus 16:16 (NAB)
[72] Exodus 16:20 (NAB)

[73] Exodus 16:22 (NAB)
[74] Exodus 16:26 (NAB)
[75] Exodus 16:28 (NAB)
[76] Angie O'Gorman, What's the manna?, National Catholic Reporter, 21 June 2014, https://www.ncronline.org/blogs/spiritual-reflections/whats-manna, (accessed 12 April 2024)
[77] Meriam-Webster, Community, https://www.merriam-webster.com/dictionary/community, (accessed 12 April 2024)
[78] Angie O'Gorman, What's the manna?, National Catholic Reporter, 21 June 2014, https://www.ncronline.org/blogs/spiritual-reflections/whats-manna, (accessed 13 April 2024)
[79] Deuteronomy 8:2 (NAB)
[80] Exodus 14:6-9 (NAB)
[81] Exodus 14:11-12 (NAB)
[82] Exodus 14:20 (NAB)
[83] Exodus 14:21 (NAB)
[84] Exodus 14:28 (NAB)
[85] Exodus 14:30 (NAB)
[86] Exodus 16:12 (NAB)
[87] Catechism of the Catholic Church, Second Edition, Section 1324
[88] Ariel Ben Ami, Catholics for Israel on Understanding the Temple: Jerusalem in the Time of Jesus, *Travel & Leisure – Catholic Online*, 27 March 2012, https://www.catholic.org/travel/story.php?id=45366, (accessed 23 April 2024)
[89] 2 Chronicles 1:3-6 (NAB)
[90] 2 Chronicles 1:7-12 (NAB)
[91] 2 Chronicles 2:4-5 (NAB)
[92] 2 Chronicles 2:12-17 (NAB)
[93] King Solomon: A Divine Wisdom and Flawed Legacy, *Young Catholics*, https://young-catholics.com/50916/king-solomon-divine-wisdom-flawed-legacy/, (accessed 27 April 2024)

[94] 2 Chronicles, Commentary, Winfried Corduan, TGCBC, https://www.thegospelcoalition.org/commentary/2-chronicles/#section-12, (accessed 21 April 2024)
[95] 2 Chronicles 3:10-14 (NAB)
[96] 2 Chronicles 4:19-22 (NAB)
[97] Hebrews 9:4 (NAB)
[98] Exodus 32:25-29 (NAB)
[99] 2 Chronicles 5:11-14 (NAB)

[100] 2 Chronicles 6:1-40 (NAB)
[101] 2 Chronicles 7:1-5 (NAB)
[102] 2 Chronicles 6:33 (NAB)
[103] Ahab, Encyclopedia Britannica, 7 February 2024, https://www.britannica.com/biography/Ahab, (accessed 12 July 2024)
[104] Ahab, Wikipedia, https://en.wikipedia.org/wiki/Ahab#:~:text=Ahab%20became%20king%20of%20Israel,the%20dates%20874%E2%80%93853%20BC., (accessed 12 July 2024)
[105] 1 Kings 16:30 (NAB)
[106] Ahab, Wikipedia, https://en.wikipedia.org/wiki/Ahab#:~:text=Ahab%20became%20king%20of%20Israel,the%20dates%20874%E2%80%93853%20BC., (accessed 12 July 2024)
[107] Elijah, Encyclopedia Britannica, 20 June 2024, https://www.britannica.com/biography/Elijah-Hebrew-prophet, (accessed 12 July 2024)
[108] 1Kings 17:2-9 (NAB)
[109] 1 Kings 17:17-24 (NAB)
[110] 1 Kings 18:1-20 (NAB)
[111] 1 Kings 18:21-24 (NAB)
[112] 1 Kings 18:25-29 (NAB)
[113] 1Kings 18:30-33 (NAB)
[114] 1Kings 18:38-39 (NAB)
[115] 1Kings 18:40-46 (NAB)
[116] 1Kings 19:1-2 (NAB)
[117] Matthew 17:2-3 (NAB)
[118] Rod Bennett, What did Jesus and Moses talk about at the Transfiguration?, *Catholic Answers Magazine*, 14 March 2022, https://www.catholic.com/magazine/online-edition/what-did-jesus-and-moses-talk-about-at-the-transfiguration, (accessed 15 July 2024)
[119] What was the meaning and importance of the Transfiguration?, *GotQuestions.org*, https://www.gotquestions.org/transfiguration.html, (accessed 15 July 2024)
[120] 2Kings 2:11-12 (NAB)
[121] 1Kings 19:4 (NAB)
[122] 1Kings 19:5-6 (NAB)
[123] 1Kings 19:7 (NAB)
[124] 1Kings 19:8 (NAB)
[125] 1Kings 19:9-10 (NAB)

[126] 1Kings 19:11 (NAB)
[127] 1Kings 19:11-12 (NAB)
[128] 1Kings 19:13-18 (NAB)
[129] Catechism of the Catholic Church, Second Edition, Part 2, Article 3, Section 1324
[130] Wikipedia, Bethlehem, Section – Classical Period, https://en.wikipedia.org/wiki/Bethlehem, (accessed 21 July 2024)
[131] Bethlehem, The Amazing name Bethlehem: Meaning & Etymology, *Abarim Publications*, https://www.abarim-publications.com/Meaning/Bethlehem.html, (accessed 21 July 2024
[132] Father Patrick Briscoe, Discovering the Eucharist at Bethlehem, *Our Sunday Visitor*, 20 December 2022, https://www.oursundayvisitor.com/discovering-the-eucharist-at-bethlehem/, (accessed 21 July 2024)
[133] What is the Importance of Bethlehem in the Bible?, *GotQuestions.org*, https://www.gotquestions.org/Bethlehem-in-the-Bible.html, (accessed 21 July 2024)
[134] Bethlehem Meaning – Bible Definition and References, *Easton's Bible Dictionary* – Bethlehem, https://www.biblestudytools.com/dictionary/bethlehem/#:~:text=Easton's%20Bible%20Dictionary%20%2D%20Bethlehem,%3B%20Ruth%204%3A11%20)., (accessed 21 July 2024)
[135] 1 Samuel 16:4-13 (NAB)
[136] Wikipedia, Ephrath, https://en.wikipedia.org/wiki/Ephrath, (accessed 21 July 2024) – also Genesis 35:16-19 (NAB)
[137] Ruth 2:1-23 (NAB)
[138] Matthew 1:5 (NAB)
[139] Bethlehem – Messiah's birthplace: A detailed look at Micah 5:1-2 and some objections that skeptics have, AboutBibleProphecy.com, http://www.aboutbibleprophecy.com/bethlehem.htm, (accessed 22 July 2024)
[140] Felix Just, S.J., Ph.D., The Birth of Jesus: Comparing the Gospel Infancy Narratives, *Catholic-Resources.org*, https://catholic-resources.org/Bible/Jesus-Birth.htm, (accessed 22 July 2024)
[141] Felix Just, S.J., Ph.D., The Birth of Jesus: Comparing the Gospel Infancy Narratives, *Catholic-Resources.org*, https://catholic-resources.org/Bible/Jesus-Birth.htm, (accessed 22 July 2024)
[142] Matthew 2:1-6 (NAB)

[143] Summa Theologica, Third Part, Article 7, Whether Christ should have been born in Bethlehem?, https://www.ccel.org/ccel/aquinas/summa.TP_Q35_A7.html, (accessed 22 July 2024)

[144] Pope Saint John Paul II, homily for Midnight Mass 2004, found in the article by Father Patric Briscoe, Discovering the Eucharist at Bethlehem, 20 December 2022, https://www.oursundayvisitor.com/discovering-the-eucharist-at-bethlehem/#:~:text=In%20Bethlehem%20was%20born%20the,which%20gives%20life%20to%20humanity., (accessed 23 July 2024)

[145] John 6:55-56 (NAB)

[146] Luke 2:7 (NAB)

[147] Manger Definition & Meaning, Merriam-Webster, https://www.merriam-webster.com/dictionary/manger, (accessed 23 July 2024)

[148] Isaiah 1:3 (NAB)

[149] Father Patrick Briscoe, Discovering the Eucharist at Bethlehem, *Our Sunday Visitor*, 20 December 2022, https://www.oursundayvisitor.com/discovering-the-eucharist-at-bethlehem/, (accessed 21 July 2024)

[150] Bethlehem, Easton's Bible Dictionary, https://www.biblestudytools.com/dictionaries/eastons-bible-dictionary/bethlehem.html, (accessed 23 July 2024)

[151] Wikipedia, Church of the Nativity, https://en.wikipedia.org/wiki/Church_of_the_Nativity, (accessed 23 July 2024)

[152] David Asher, Spiritual Meaning of Bethlehem – Significance of the Place, *Elijah Tours*, 25 February 2020, https://elijahtours.com/blogs/articles/spiritual-meaning-of-bethlehem-significance-of-the-place, (accessed 23 July 2024)

[153] Wikipedia, Church of the Nativity, https://en.wikipedia.org/wiki/Church_of_the_Nativity, (accessed 23 July 2024)

[154] Saint Leo History, https://www.saintleoabbey.org/st-leo-history, (accessed 24 July 2024)

[155] Luke 2:10 (NAB)

[156] Luke 2:12 (NAB)

[157] Luke 2:13-14 (NAB)

[158] What were common marriage customs in Bible Times?, GotQuestions.org, https://www.gotquestions.org/marriage-customs.html, (accessed 27 July 2024)

[159] Steve Rudd, Marriage in the Bible and Ancient Marriage and Jewish Wedding Customs, https://www.bible.ca/marriage/ancient-jewish-three-stage-weddings-and-marriage-customs-ceremony-in-the-bible.htm, (accessed 28 July 2024)

[160] Steve Rudd, Marriage in the Bible and Ancient Marriage and Jewish Wedding Customs, https://www.bible.ca/marriage/ancient-jewish-three-stage-weddings-and-marriage-customs-ceremony-in-the-bible.htm, (accessed 28 July 2024)

[161] Monsignor Charles Pope, What were weddings like in Jesus' day?, *Community in Mission*, 13 August 2014, https://blog.adw.org/2014/08/what-were-weddings-like-in-jesus-day/#:~:text=Usually%20the%20entire%20village%20gathered,and%20sometimes%20even%20a%20crown., (accessed 28 July 2024)

[162] Steve Rudd, Marriage in the Bible and Ancient Marriage and Jewish Wedding Customs, https://www.bible.ca/marriage/ancient-jewish-three-stage-weddings-and-marriage-customs-ceremony-in-the-bible.htm, (accessed 28 July 2024)

[163] What were common marriage customs in Bible Times?, GotQuestions.org, https://www.gotquestions.org/marriage-customs.html, (accessed 27 July 2024)

[164] Steve Rudd, Marriage in the Bible and Ancient Marriage and Jewish Wedding Customs, https://www.bible.ca/marriage/ancient-jewish-three-stage-weddings-and-marriage-customs-ceremony-in-the-bible.htm, (accessed 28 July 2024)

[165] Wikipedia, Chuppah, https://en.wikipedia.org/wiki/Chuppah#:~:text=In%20Biblical%20times%2C%20a%20couple,consummated%20was%20called%20the%20chuppah., (accessed 28 July 2024)

[166] Steve Rudd, Marriage in the Bible and Ancient Marriage and Jewish Wedding Customs, https://www.bible.ca/marriage/ancient-jewish-three-stage-weddings-and-marriage-customs-ceremony-in-the-bible.htm, (accessed 28 July 2024)

[167] Genesis 24:4 (NAB)

[168] Genesis 24:33-66 (NAB)

[169] Genesis 29:14-30 (NAB)

[170] John 2:1-3 (NAB)

[171] Genesis 27:28 (NAB)

[172] Mary Fairchild, Is there Wine in the Bible?, *Learn Religions*, 28 February 2022, https://www.learnreligions.com/is-there-wine-in-the-bible-5217794#:~:text=Mary%20Fairchild%20is%20a%20full,including%20%22Stories%20of%20Calvary.%22&text=Wine%20plays%20a%20significant%20role,delicious%20fruit%20of%20the%20vine., (accessed 29 July 2024)

[173] Zachary Garris, To Gladden the Heart of Man: A Biblical Theology of Wine, *Knowing Scripture*, 16 October 2018, https://knowingscripture.com/articles/to-gladden-the-heart-of-man-a-biblical-theology-of-wine, (accessed 29 July 2028)

[174] Father Satish Joseph, Multiplication of Loaves and Fish: A Miracle Within the Miracle, Where Peter Is, 2 August 2020, https://wherepeteris.com/multiplication-of-loaves-and-fish-a-miracle-within-the-miracle/, (accessed 3 August 2024)

[175] Commentary on the Gospel: The Loaves and Fishes, Opus Dei, https://opusdei.org/en-us/gospel/commentary-on-the-gospel-the-loaves-and-the-fish/, (accessed 3 August 2024)

[176] Matthew 14:16 (NAB)

[177] Matthew 14:17 (NAB)

[178] Matthew 14:19 (NAB)

[179] Father Satish Joseph, Multiplication of Loaves and Fish: A Miracle Within the Miracle, *Where Peter Is*, 2 August 2020, https://wherepeteris.com/multiplication-of-loaves-and-fish-a-miracle-within-the-miracle/, (accessed 3 August 2024)

[180] Father Satish Joseph, Multiplication of Loaves and Fish: A Miracle Within the Miracle, *Where Peter Is*, 2 August 2020, https://wherepeteris.com/multiplication-of-loaves-and-fish-a-miracle-within-the-miracle/, (accessed 3 August 2024)

[181] Commentary on the Gospel: The Loaves and Fishes, Opus Dei, https://opusdei.org/en-us/gospel/commentary-on-the-gospel-the-loaves-and-the-fish/, (accessed 3 August 2024)

[182] Father Satish Joseph, Multiplication of Loaves and Fish: A Miracle Within the Miracle, *Where Peter Is*, 2 August 2020, https://wherepeteris.com/multiplication-of-loaves-and-fish-a-miracle-within-the-miracle/, (accessed 3 August 2024)

[183] John 6:5-7 (NAB)

[184] John 6:8-9 (NAB)

[185] John 6:10 (NAB)

[186] John 6:10 (NKJ)
[187] Table Manners and Christianity, *Alimentarium*, https://www.alimentarium.org/en/fact-sheet/table-manners-and-christianity#:~:text=During%20Jesus'%20time%2C%20lying%20down%20to%20eat,Phoenician%20and%20Aramaic%20princes%20(populations%20of%20modern, (accessed 4 August 2024)
[188] John 6:11 (NAB)
[189] Donagh O'Shea, The Multiplication of the Loaves and Fish, *Good News*, https://www.goodnews.ie/multiplicationloavesfish.shtml, (accessed 4 August 2024)
[190] Father Daniel Callam, The Gospel of Mark: The Multiplication of the Loaves, *Catholic Insight*, 31 January 2021, https://catholicinsight.com/the-gospel-of-mark-the-multiplication-of-the-loaves/, (accessed 4 August 2024)
[191] Mark 5:43 (NAB)
[192] Mark 6:37 (NAB)
[193] [193] Father Daniel Callam, The Gospel of Mark: The Multiplication of the Loaves, *Catholic Insight*, 31 January 2021, https://catholicinsight.com/the-gospel-of-mark-the-multiplication-of-the-loaves/, (accessed 4 August 2024)
[194] The Multiplication of the Loaves, *Lo & Behold*, https://loandbeholdbible.com/2017/11/19/the-multiplication-of-the-loaves-john-61-15/#:~:text=The%20five%20loaves%20symbolised%20the,cf%20Acts%207%3A8)., (accessed 4 August 2021
[195] Father Daniel Callam, The Gospel of Mark: The Multiplication of the Loaves, *Catholic Insight*, 31 January 2021, https://catholicinsight.com/the-gospel-of-mark-the-multiplication-of-the-loaves/, (accessed 4 August 2024)
[196] Father Daniel Callam, The Gospel of Mark: The Multiplication of the Loaves, *Catholic Insight*, 31 January 2021, https://catholicinsight.com/the-gospel-of-mark-the-multiplication-of-the-loaves/, (accessed 4 August 2024)
[197] Mark 8:14 (NAB)
[198] 1Corinthians 10:17 (NAB)
[199] Father Daniel Callam, The Gospel of Mark: The Multiplication of the Loaves, *Catholic Insight*, 31 January 2021, https://catholicinsight.com/the-gospel-of-mark-the-multiplication-of-the-loaves/, (accessed 4 August 2024)

[200] Catholic Catechism, Second Edition, Section 1335 (accessed 4 August 2024)
[201] Genesis 26:4 (NAB)
[202] John 6:14 (NAB)
[203] John 6:15 (NAB)
[204] Mark 6:46 (NAB)
[205] Being Called Up the Mountain with Jesus, *Catholic Daily Reflections*, 24 January 2020, https://catholic-daily-reflections.com/2020/01/23/being-called-up-the-mountain-with-jesus/, (accessed 7 August 2024)
[206] David Platt, A Different King, *Radical*, 16 March 2023, https://radical.net/podcasts/pray-the-word/a-different-king-john-615/, (accessed 7 August 2024)
[207] Terry Storch, John 6:15 – Retreat into the mountains, 21 August 2020, https://terrystorch.com/writing/john-6-retreat-into-the-mountains, (accessed 7 August 2024)
[208] John 6:16 (NAB)
[209] John 6:19 (NAB)
[210] John 6:21 (NAB)
[211] John 6:67 (NAB)
[212] John 6:68-69 (NAB)
[213] John 6:70 (NAB)
[214] Timothy O'Malley, The Theological Foundations of Eucharistic Beliefs: A New National Survey of Adult Catholics, *Catholic Life Journal*, 6 October 2023, https://churchlifejournal.nd.edu/articles/the-theological-foundations-of-eucharistic-beliefs-a-national-survey-of-adult-catholics/#:~:text=The%20Eucharist%20is%20the%20true,us%2C%20feeding%20us%20with%20himself., (accessed 10 August 2024)
[215] Jonah McKeown, New study suggest more than two-thirds of Catholics believe the Eucharist is truly Jesus, *Catholic News Agency*, 16 June 2024, https://www.catholicnewsagency.com/news/258013/new-study-suggests-more-than-two-thirds-of-catholics-believe-the-eucharist-is-truly-jesus, (accessed 10 August 2024)
[216] Francis J. Ripley, Transubstantiation for Beginners, *Catholic Answers*, 1 July 1993, https://www.catholic.com/magazine/print-edition/transubstantiation-for-beginners, (accessed 11 August 2024)
[217] Matthew 26:17 (NAB)
[218] John 6:51 (NAB)
[219] Luke 22:19 (NAB)
[220] John 6:53-56 (NAB)

[221] Old versus new covenant, St. Luke the Evangelist Catholic Church, Slidell, LA, 28 March 2015, https://saintlukeslidell.org/news/old-versus-new-covenant, (accessed 11 August 2024)

[222] Father Charles Grondin, How Many Covenants Are There in the Bible?, *Catholic Answers*, https://www.catholic.com/qa/how-many-covenants-are-there-in-the-bible, (accessed 11 August 2024)

[223] Luke 22:19 (NAB)

[224] Francis J. Ripley, Transubstantiation for Beginners, *Catholic Answers*, 1 July 1993, https://www.catholic.com/magazine/print-edition/transubstantiation-for-beginners, (accessed 11 August 2024)

[225] The Eucharist, USCCB, https://www.usccb.org/eucharist, (accessed 11 August 2024)

[226] John 6:68-69 (NAB)

[227] Luke 22:10 (NAB)

[228] Luke 22:11 (NAB)

[229] Passover in the Time of Jesus, https://bible.org/article/passover-time-jesus, (accessed 13 August 2024)

[230] Passover in the Time of Jesus, https://bible.org/article/passover-time-jesus, (accessed 13 August 2024)

[231] Brenna Houck, Everything You Need to Know About Charoset – a Passover Tradition, *Eater*, 7 April 2017, https://www.eater.com/2016/4/23/11477536/what-is-charoset-passover-seder, (accessed 13 August 2024)

[232] Rabbi Benjamin Elton, The mystery of the 'charoset' and the sweet legacy of Passover, *ABC Religion & Ethics*, 3 April 2023, https://www.abc.net.au/religion/rabbi-benjamin-elton-passover-mystery-of-charoset/102184644, (accessed 13 August 2024)

[233] Luke 22:15-16 (NAB)

[234] Luke 22:19 (NAB)

[235] John 6:51 (NAB)

[236] Luke 22:20 (NAB)

[237] John 19:39 (NAB)

[238] John 19:25-27 (NAB)

[239] John 19:23 (NAB)

[240] Byron R. McCane, Burial Practices in First Century Palestine, *Bible Odyssey*, https://theturkeytraveler.bibleodyssey.org/articles/burial-practices-in-first-century-palestine/#:~:text=According%20to%20the%20third%2Dcentury,bound%20in%20strips%20of%20cloth., (accessed 2 September 2024)

[241] When Did Jesus Die?, *University of Chicago*, https://penelope.uchicago.edu/~grout/encyclopaedia_romana/calendar/jesus.html#:~:text=The%20Gospels%20all%20agree%20that,37)%2C%20when%20Pontius%20Pilate%20was, (accessed 2 September 2024)
[242] Life of Jesus Christ by Anne Catherine Emmerich, Document ACE_4_0321, https://tandfspi.org/ACE_vol_04/ACE_4_0321_out.html, (accessed 2 September 2024)
[243] Luke 23:55-56; 24:1 (NAB)
[244] What was the significance of anointing spices in the Bible?, *Got Questions.org*, https://www.gotquestions.org/anointing-spices.html, (accessed 2 September 2024)
[245] Luke 24:3 (NAB)
[246] Luke 24:4-9 (NAB)
[247] Luke 24:11-12 (NAB)
[248] Luke 24:15-16 (NAB)
[249] John 20:1-2 (NAB)
[250] John 20:11-12 (NAB)
[251] John 20:13 (NAB)
[252] John 20:15 (NAB)
[253] John 20:15 (NAB)
[254] John 20:16 (NAB)
[255] Dave Armstrong, 12 Alleged Resurrection "Contradictions" that Aren't Really Contradictions, *National Catholic Register*, 7 April 2021, https://www.ncregister.com/blog/12-alleged-resurrection-contradictions, (accessed 3 September 2024)
[256] Dr. Tim Chaffey, Christ's Resurrection – Four Accounts, One Reality, *Answers Magazine*, https://answersingenesis.org/jesus/resurrection/christs-resurrection-four-accounts-one-reality/, (accessed 3 September 2024)
[257] Dr. Tim Chaffey, Christ's Resurrection – Four Accounts, One Reality, *Answers Magazine*, https://answersingenesis.org/jesus/resurrection/christs-resurrection-four-accounts-one-reality/, (accessed 3 September 2024)
[258] Luke 24:28 (NAB)
[259] Luke 24:30-31 (NAB)
[260] Luke 24:34 (NAB)
[261] Luke 24:35 (NAB)
[262] Catechism of the Catholic Church, Second Edition, Section 205, (accessed 3 September 2024)

[263] Stephen M. Barr, St. Augustine's Relativistic Theory of Time, *Church Life Journal*, 7 February 2020, https://churchlifejournal.nd.edu/articles/augustines-push-against-the-limits-of-time/, (accessed 3 September 2024)

[264] Stephen M. Barr, St. Augustine's Relativistic Theory of Time, *Church Life Journal*, 7 February 2020, https://churchlifejournal.nd.edu/articles/augustines-push-against-the-limits-of-time/, (accessed 3 September 2024)

[265] Reverend Stephen Grunow, Introduction to Revelation, *The Word on Fire Bible – Acts, Letters, and Revelation*, Printed and bound in Italy 2022, page 718 to 720

[266] Reverend Stephen Grunow, Introduction to Revelation, *The Word on Fire Bible – Acts, Letters, and Revelation*, Printed and bound in Italy 2022, page 718 to 720

[267] The Catholic Study Bible, Second Edition, *New American Bible Revised Edition*, Oxford University Press 2011, page 1752 to 1753

[268] Bishop Robert Barron, The Marriage Supper of the Lamb, *The Word on Fire Bible – Acts, Letters, and Revelation*, Printed and bound in Italy 2022, page 799

[269] Dr. Edward Sri, The Wedding Supper of the Lamb, *Ascension Press Media*, https://media.ascensionpress.com/podcast/the-wedding-supper-of-the-lamb/, (accessed 4 September 2024)

[270] Scott Hahn, The Supper of the Lamb, *St. Paul Center*, 31 October 2011, https://stpaulcenter.com/the-supper-of-the-lamb/, (accessed 4 September 2024)

[271] Mark Shea, Eucharist: The Marriage Supper of the Lamb, *National Catholic Register*, 9 February 2010, https://www.ncregister.com/blog/eucharist-the-marriage-supper-of-the-lamb, (accessed 5 September 2024)

[272] Mark Shea, Eucharist: The Marriage Supper of the Lamb, *National Catholic Register*, 9 February 2010, https://www.ncregister.com/blog/eucharist-the-marriage-supper-of-the-lamb, (accessed 5 September 2024)

[273] Pedro A. Moreno, O.P., Our wedding feast with Christ!, Archdiocese of Oklahoma City, Oklahoma City, OK, 7 May 2020, https://archokc.org/news/our-wedding-feast-with-christ, (accessed 5 September 2024)

[274] Catechism of the Catholic Church, Second Edition, Section 1404, https://www.usccb.org/sites/default/files/flipbooks/catechism/356/, (accessed 5 September 2024)

[275] Eamon Tobin, 13 Powerful Ways to Pray, *DynamicCatholics.com*, Wellspring 2016, Chapter 5: Prayer of Forgiveness, page 109 to 112

[276] Father John A. Hardon, S.J., Eucharistic Saints, *Catholic Culture*, https://www.catholicculture.org/culture/library/view.cfm?id=6313#:~:text=Ignatius%20of%20Antioch%2C%20St.,words%20of%20consecration%20at%20Mass., (accessed 8 September 2024)

[277] Eleven saint quotes on the eucharist for Corpus Christi Sunday, *Catholic News Agency*, 19 June 2022, https://catholicleader.com.au/life/faith/eleven-saint-quotes-on-the-eucharist-for-corpus-christi-sunday/, (accessed 8 September 2024)

[278] Saint Francis de Sales, The Catholic Controversy – A Defense of the Faith, Published by Burns and Oates, London and by Catholic Publication Society Co., New York in 1886, Reprinted by TAN Books in 1989, back cover, (accessed 8 September 2024)

[279] Eleven saint quotes on the eucharist for Corpus Christi Sunday, *Catholic News Agency*, 19 June 2022, https://catholicleader.com.au/life/faith/eleven-saint-quotes-on-the-eucharist-for-corpus-christi-sunday/, (accessed 8 September 2024)

[280] Eleven saint quotes on the eucharist for Corpus Christi Sunday, *Catholic News Agency*, 19 June 2022, https://catholicleader.com.au/life/faith/eleven-saint-quotes-on-the-eucharist-for-corpus-christi-sunday/, (accessed 8 September 2024)

[281] Francesca Pollio Fenton, Courtney Mares, 10 Things you Should Know about Blessed Carlo Acutis, Catholic News Agency, 23 May 2024, https://www.catholicnewsagency.com/news/46048/who-was-carlo-acutis-a-cna-explainer, (accessed 8 September 2024)

[282] Francesca Pollio Fenton, Courtney Mares, 10 Things you Should Know about Blessed Carlo Acutis, Catholic News Agency, 23 May 2024, https://www.catholicnewsagency.com/news/46048/who-was-carlo-acutis-a-cna-explainer, (accessed 8 September 2024)

[283] Francesca Pollio Fenton, Courtney Mares, 10 Things you Should Know about Blessed Carlo Acutis, Catholic News Agency, 23 May 2024, https://www.catholicnewsagency.com/news/46048/who-was-carlo-acutis-a-cna-explainer, (accessed 8 September 2024)

[284] Miracles List – The Eucharistic Miracles of the World, An International Exhibition designed and created by Carlo Acutis – the Servant of God, Buenos Aires, Argentina,

http://www.miracolieucaristici.org/en/Liste/scheda_c.html?nat=argentina&wh=buenosaires&ct=Buenos%20Aires,%201992-1994-1996, (accessed 8 September 2024)

[285] The Guardian Angel: Eucharistic Miracle Chirattakonam, India, Deeper Truth Blog, https://www.deepertruthcatholics.com/single-post/the-guardian-angel-eucharistic-miracle-chirattakonam-india, (accessed 9 September 2024)

[286] Miracles List – The Eucharist Miracles of the World, An International Exhibition designed and created by Carlo Acutis – the Servant of God, India, http://www.miracolieucaristici.org/en/Liste/scheda.html?nat=india&wh=chirattakonam&ct=Chirattakonam,%202001, (accessed 8 September 2024)

[287] Father Rober J. Spitzer, S.J., 4 Approved Eucharistic Miracles from the 21st Century, Magis Center, 31 August 2020, https://www.magiscenter.com/blog/approved-eucharistic-miracles-21st-century, (accessed 8 September 2024)

[288] Blog: Updates and Inspiration from the Revival, National Eucharistic Revival Prayer, 5 June 2023, https://www.eucharisticrevival.org/post/national-eucharistic-revival-prayer#:~:text=%E2%80%8D,come%20and%20love%20in%20me., (accessed 8 September 2024)

Made in the USA
Middletown, DE
15 February 2025